Edward Sandford Martin

Cousin Anthony and I

Some Views of ours about Divers Matters and Various Aspects of Life

Edward Sandford Martin

Cousin Anthony and I
Some Views of ours about Divers Matters and Various Aspects of Life

ISBN/EAN: 9783337778033

Printed in Europe, USA, Canada, Australia, Japan

Cover: Foto ©Thomas Meinert / pixelio.de

More available books at **www.hansebooks.com**

COUSIN ANTHONY
AND I

COUSIN ANTHONY AND I;

SOME VIEWS OF OURS

ABOUT DIVERS MATTERS

AND

VARIOUS ASPECTS OF LIFE

BY

EDWARD SANDFORD MARTIN

AUTHOR OF "A LITTLE BROTHER OF THE RICH"
AND "WINDFALLS OF OBSERVATION"

NEW YORK
CHARLES SCRIBNER'S SONS
1895

COPYRIGHT, 1895, BY
CHARLES SCRIBNER'S SONS

TROW DIRECTORY
PRINTING AND BOOKBINDING COMPANY
NEW YORK

INSCRIBED,

WITH AFFECTION AND RESPECT,

TO

THAT ADMIRABLE WOMAN,

MY COUSIN ANTHONY'S WIFE

CONTENTS

		PAGE
I.	Cousin Anthony and His Book	1
II.	Readers and Reading	15
III.	Work and the Yankee	29
IV.	Chores	41
V.	Considerations Matrimonial	53
VI.	Love, Friendship, and Gossip	73
VII.	Woman Suffrage	89
VIII.	The Knowledge of Good and Evil	103
IX.	Civilization and Culture	119
X.	Arcadia and Belgravia	137
XI.	Ourselves and Other People	157
XII.	Profit and Loss	177
XIII.	Certain Assets of Age	193
XIV.	The After-Dinner Speech	203
XV.	Cousin Anthony's Address to the Trained Nurses	213

⁎ *Acknowledgment is made of the courtesy of the proprietors of* SCRIBNER'S MAGAZINE, HARPER'S WEEKLY, THE NORTH AMERICAN REVIEW, *and* THE SUN *for permission to include in this volume articles contributed to those publications.*

1
COUSIN ANTHONY AND HIS BOOK

COUSIN ANTHONY AND HIS BOOK

Y Cousin Anthony was lately speaking of the surprised respect he sometimes felt for himself because of certain things he had not said. He went a little into details, and I discovered that nearly all the unutterances that he prided himself upon were things that he had omitted to tell his wife. He felt, he said, that not to blurt out matters to the general public is no particular credit to a man, but the inducement to tell one's wife everything that would interest her is so strong that to have restrained one's self from the abuse of such a privilege is fair ground for humble self-approbation. There are things that a conscientious man does not feel authorized to admit even to himself. A fact that is not admitted is more

Discreet reticence of my cousin.

or less ineffectual. It may have a potentiality of mischief about it and still be harmless so long as it is ignored. To know something that is disquieting to one's self to know, and to let it die of neglect, is sane conduct; and so it is to know something that would worry one's wife and to abstain from imparting it to her because it is wholly unnecessary for her to know it.

At least that was the view that my cousin Anthony took. He maintained that to confide absolutely in one's wife was indeed good, but to temper candor on occasion with a wise and affectionate reticence was better still. He by no means advocated deceit or elaborate concealment. He hates a lie as much as anyone, and is as eager as Merlin himself to have vinegar burned when there is a liar to the windward. But mere abstention from inconsiderate admissions he admired in himself.

I think he is right. Confession may be good for the soul, but a Protestant who employs no professional confessor is bound to consider how his outpourings will affect the ear they enter. Let him steer them into an ear that they are sure to pass through, and not into one where they may stick and rankle.

Anthony says that he never descants to his wife about any callow preliminary affair of the heart that he was ever involved in. She had shown, he said, a benevolent willingness to hear and sympathize with his experiences of that sort; but though not to tell her involved the suppression of some of the most interesting tales he knew, some saving grace of marital circumspection had achieved the suppression. What biographical details of that sort came to her from other authorities than himself gave him not the slightest concern. There was a wide distinction, according to his notion, between the information that she took the responsibility of acquiring and that which he took the responsibility of forcing upon her attention.

Another class of information that he systematically omits to share with her includes all gossip which comes to his ears that is derogatory to her own family. As he thinks it unwise to tell her things that might make her think less of him, so he omits information that might make her think less of herself. He told me a tale about his wife's uncle, Philip Hiram, that was really of the liveliest interest even to a stranger. But he said he had never told it to his wife, because it would mortify her to know it, and as no one but himself would dare tell her, the chances were that she would never hear it.

· Anthony does not think himself a sly dog for not telling everything to Mrs. Anthony. To his mind his reticence shows not his doubts of his wife's discretion or regard, but his sedulous regard for her happiness and the high value he places on her affection. Those are things of too much importance to put to hazard by impulsive revelations. He is really exceptionally frank in his ordinary communications, and to know anything that is worth telling and not to tell it is a sort of self-sacrifice that no one who knows him would expect of him. Least of all did he expect it of himself. He simply found that there were a few things that he was periodically tempted

Cousin Anthony and His Book

to tell, and didn't tell, and was always surprised afterward that he hadn't.

But Anthony is not so marvellously discreet about everything. Without being morbid he is one of those introspective creatures who sort out their own blemishes and misdemeanors and repent of them after they are all good and done. He writes as well as talks, and perhaps he has less occasion to felicitate himself on what he has left unwritten than on the things he has not said. It happens that way sometimes, that men who are the carefullest and most continent in their talk are subject to extraordinary bursts of candor with a pen and ink. But as I said Anthony writes things, and had the felicity, not a great while since, to compose a book which so stirred the benevolence of his friends that he has complained to me of the embarrassment their praises have caused him. He declares that if the book were really very much of a book he wouldn't mind its being praised, but being merely such a book as he knows it is, and containing only such things as he managed to get into it, the assurances that

The book he wrote.

he gets of its merits make him feel like a receiver of stolen goods, and seem to him a design of the Arch Enemy to bring him low. If he didn't like it, he says, he would be less disturbed; but there is evidence that his receivership is all too agreeable to him.

I have tried to console him as far as I could, pointing out to him that in every enterprise one is bound to take the evil with the good, and that if the book is good enough to praise it may be good enough to sell. Furthermore, I have suggested to him that his excessive aspiration after humility is itself a symptom of spiritual pride, and that it may really be wiser to let his poor head swell and cure itself by natural processes than to worry unduly over it and try to keep it down by artificial means. A good many people, I tell him, have time on their hands in these days, and some one will find leisure presently to read his poor book through, and find out how little, after all, there is in it. The cure in such cases often comes that way. Besides, I have pointed out to him, what he should have known himself, that it is a great mistake to suppose that there is nothing in a book except what the writer puts there. There is something at Rome, but the more important part is what you take there; and what the reader is able to get out of any book depends very considerably, of course, upon what he brings to it. If one is long of steel it is great luck to run across a bed of flints, but there is no occasion for the steel to assume all the responsibility for the resulting sparks.

I think I will read cousin Anthony's book myself, presently, and see if there is really any good in it. There may be. The fact that his friends praise it is not proof that there is, but neither is it proof to the contrary. But, as I told him, even if it is good it is nothing to be so swollen over. If a boy can fly a kite, it is a good sport. Let him practise it and take pleasure in it. But it is the wind that does the work, not he; moreover, it is the kite that flies and not the boy, so that for him to imagine himself afloat, and impart wing-movements to his members, is an absurdity of self-deception.

Let the kite be puffed up, but not the boy. "So let your book," I said, "my cousin, be borne on by any lucky gale of approbation that may come its way; without disparagement of which, be you content to hold the string and run with it when necessary. That is the business of a writer, not to fly himself, but to send up good kites, and make the wind carry them. If anyone have the faculty to recognize a certain measure of truth and so to work it up that it will go, and that others may know it when they see it, let him do so, for it is a good thing. But as for being personally inflated about it, that is folly, for it is not the writer who is glorious, but the truth, and truth was there before he found it."

The great literary advantage

I WONDER if persons who can write Scotch are sufficiently aware of the great literary advantage they have over writers who are not born to that ability. It is no credit to them that they can do it. It is a gift of nature dropt in their lap. I never heard of anyone who learned by artificial means to write Scotch. Scotch writers do it, and no one else. It has long been obvious that the proportion of good writers to the whole Scotch population was exceedingly large; but I do not remember that it has ever been pointed out how much easier it is for a Scotchman to be a good writer than another because of his innate command of the Scotch tongue.

There are such delightful words in that language; words that sing on the printed page wherever their employer happens to drop them in; words that rustle; words that skirl, and words that clash and thump. It is their gain, I believe, that not many of us who know the sounds of them have an accurate notion of their meanings. Do you know what a brae is? After thirty years of familiarity with that word I am still a little dubious about it and cannot be sure whether the idea it conveys contains underbrush or is open field, and if the latter, whether there is an implication of heather. Perhaps sheep graze on braes. I could not be sure, and if a well-informed person insisted that Scotch nosegays had braes in them I could not contradict him with much confidence. But for all that

Ye banks and braes o' Bonny Doon

conveys an image as delightful to my mind's eye as to the actual ear, and what uncertainty there may be about the dimensions and ingredients of the braes in it merely operates to give the imagination greater scope. I can aver that at least one habitual reader of English finds his attention curiously and agreeably quickened by Scotch words and idioms that are familiar enough not to be troublesome, and unfamiliar enough to give the ear a gentle fillip. A brook sparkles brighter for the moment for being a burn; "gone gyte" makes a prompter conveyance of its significance than "gone crazy;" brogues and lugs and bairns fit better into many sentences than shoes and ears and children. "A wheen blethers" fills the mouth like a spoonful of oatmeal; "twine" is a better word than "separate;" "will can" beats "will be able," and the verb to ken in all its uses is fit to

of writing Scotch.

stir the envy of the English writer. A French word dragged into English writing is an offence which is only tolerable when a master-hand commits it and the excuse is adequate, but the Scotch words of Scotchmen vary the tongue that harbors them only to enrich it, and stand among their English cousins with all the confiding assurance of blood relations.

It is to be hoped that the Scotch writers, and especially the story-tellers, appreciate with due humility the advantage they enjoy in having unrestricted use of as much English as they can handle, and in addition a monopoly of their own blessed brogue. There is scant justice in the dispensation that secures them their special privilege. They do not need it, for many of them write just as good English as even the Americans do, and are perfectly at home in that language. There is no true propriety in granting them special rights to write Scotch and English with the same pen on the same page; but on grounds of expediency, and because the mixture makes good reading, they have been suffered to do so. I am not one of those who would abridge their privilege, for I like its results; but I do think that in consideration of their advantages Scotch writers should be humble, should make allowances for other scribes, and in all literary competitions should be handicapped down to an equality with the writers in whose field they compete.

II
READERS AND READING

READERS AND READING

ERSONS who not being, like my cousin Anthony, already in the business of writing are tempted to dabble in it, should consider, among other objections to such a course, the great detriment it may prove to their usefulness, and possibly also to their enjoyment as readers. To be a good reader is a vocation by itself, *A disability of writers.* and one which writers habitually and enviously admire. That the business of writing conflicts with it is notorious. When the library of the late Guy de Maupassant came to be examined by his executors it was found that almost all the modern books in it were gifts from the authors of them, and that their leaves were in almost every instance uncut. Writers do read books occasionally, and even books by other contemporary writers, but they usually read

them either for a special purpose, as to make a review, or with the general purpose to keep informed about what is being written, or with a certain feverish anxiety to make sure that someone else is not doing their kind of work better than they can do it themselves. Find a contemporary writer, if you can, who does not look back with regret to the time when the reading of books was an irresponsible felicity. He read " Ivanhoe " and " The Tale of Two Cities " with simple happiness and no sense of obligation to dissect the authors' art or arrive at his own critical opinions. But nowadays when he reads it is with a balance in one hand, and constant interruptions while the actual book goes into one scale and his notion of what it ought to be, or his recollection of some book someone else has written, into the other. To read books simply for what there is in them, and with no conscious regard for what one's verdict will be when the reading is over, that may be reckoned one of the joys of youth. But it is not strictly a joy that belongs to youth only, for some grown people have it too; but not (or at least very rarely) if they are writers. The spectacle of the blithe maiden in a brand-new balldress is a jocund sight, even to a dressmaker. But the dressmaker does not take the same unimpeded delight in it that it brings to the other spectators. Inevitably and unconsciously she counts the stitches, reckons the cost of the fabric, measures off in her mind the yards of lace, and appraises the quality of the trimmings; then she compares it mentally with other fine frocks, and when she has finished she knows far more about the gown than anyone who has seen it except the society reporter. But there is a quality in the pretty show that her scrutiny has missed and an emotion she has not gathered because her trained sight saw so much.

Everyone who has ever launched a book which has drifted in even a moderate degree into the current of public favor must remember how overwhelming a proportion of whatever subsequent satisfaction he got from it was due to that simple, old-fashioned, uncritical personage, the gentle reader, who reads books for the promotion of his own happiness, and if he likes them knows it and is cheerfully ready to say so. For the faults or shortcomings of a book the gentle reader doesn't much care if only there is a grace in it somewhere to which his soul responds. If it is verse, it does not concern him that Tennyson wrote better; if it is a story he does not throw it down because it is not the equal of "Vanity Fair." If it gives him real pleasure, in sufficient quantity to pay for the time he spent in reading it, he declares that it is a good book and is ready to thank the author and buy and read the next book that he sends out. He, or perhaps I should say she, is the reader that the author loves and esteems and counts upon to quiet his own literary compunctions. But the reader who has himself dabbled much in writing can seldom be a gentle reader afterward. He is always a critic, mistrusting his own pleasure and his fellow's art; hesitating to express his possible favor for fear it will discredit his own discrimination, more eager to make a clever comment of his own than to

The gentle reader.

find a pearl of someone else's thought. He has some knowledge of good and evil which the gentle reader lacks, but it is dearly bought, as perhaps all knowledge must be. To be sure, a good critic is a useful creature in his way, but it is a very good critic indeed in the making of whom it is worth while that a gentle reader should be spoiled.

Happily, in spite of the current epidemic of authorship, the gentle reader still seems to abound and to read books with uncorrupted faculties. A year or two ago a Boston newspaper of high literary responsibility chronicled the death of Mrs. So-and-so, "the distinguished author." It gave a sketch of her life and a list of her principal books. There were a baker's dozen of them, and an ink-bedabbled reader who ran his eye down the list failed to recognize a single title that he had ever heard of before. But the gentle reader must have read those books and approved them with his catholic kindness, else so many of them had never lived in print, and the good author had gone with a soul far less relieved to her honorable rest.

Cousin Anthony and I

It is surprising what readers, gentle and otherwise, are expected to accomplish, and do accomplish after a fashion, nowadays. No wonder it should be thought and often remarked that the contemporary reader is in pretty deep waters, and that doubts should be now and then expressed as to his ability to keep his head above them. A century ago there was a little library of classics that he read at more or less, and if he could lay hands on a weekly newspaper he read that too. Two generations ago he was taking a daily paper, and perhaps an eclectic magazine made up from the British monthlies. The civil war upset his habits and set him to reading all the newspapers he could afford to buy, and weekly picture-papers and a monthly magazine besides. The cheapening of the cost of white paper and the lowering of the price of "news" has confirmed him in the habits he learned then. Such an amount of reading is offered him now for two cents that he feels that he cannot afford to take in less than two or three newspapers, and the magazines are so cheap and so admirable that

Bad case of the contemporary reader.

22

Readers and Reading

he must read one or two of them every month. And all the time books keep tumbling out from the presses faster than ever, and, of course, a man who thinks that he has a mind is bound to feed it part of the time on books. No wonder that the contemporary reader is embarrassed, and complains that he cannot keep up, and wants to know what to do about it.

There is nothing more serious really the matter than that the conditions under which he is struggling are novel, and that he has not yet adapted himself to their requirements. In primitive times when men wandered about in the woods and roosted in trees at night, they ate what they could find wherever and whenever they found it. As food grew more plentiful they only ate when they were hungry, and gradually they got the habit of being hungry at stated intervals. Then as the variety of victuals increased they developed the civilized practice of using certain kinds of food for particular meals, and came gradually to the sophisticated method of having things served by courses, and varying their diet according to the hour of the day and the state of the market. No civilized New Yorker complains because there are more kinds of fish in Fulton Market than his palate can test or his stomach accommodate. If he has smelts for his breakfast and salmon after his soup at dinner, he is thankful and tries not to eat overmuch of either of them. He must teach himself to take his literature in the same enlightened manner, reading according to his appetite and his necessities, as he would eat; not gorging himself because the market is generous; not eating a pie for breakfast nor beginning his dinner with coffee, but taking things as they ought to come.

And especially, if he is an intelligent man and wants to make the most of his day, he must read his newspapers with intelligence, doing it quickly while his mind is fresh, wresting the news out of them like the meat from a nutshell, and discarding the rest. It is easy for him, if he allows himself to do so, to read the newspapers and nothing else, just as it is a simple matter to support life on hog and hominy.

But if he is going to read to the best purpose he must have a system about his reading analogous to that which regulates his diet. If he reads the newspapers as he ought to read them, and does not spend his eyes on "miscellany" and spun-out gossip, he will have time to get through them and keep the run of the magazines besides. If he reads the best of what is in the magazines he will read most of the best new fiction before it gets between covers, and will supplement usefully the current information that he gets from the newspapers. If he reads in the magazines only what appeals to him, he will still have time every day to read something in a book; and if he makes a point of reading something, however little, every day in a book that is worth reading, his library will be bound to pay him high interest on its value.

Above all things the modern must adapt his reading, in bulk and quality, to his personal circumstances and individual wants. The very multitude of new books destroys the obligation to read many of them. There is nothing any longer except the Bible and Shakespeare that the contemporary American need blush not to know. If he has intelligence and reasonable culture the presumption will be that if he has not read this it was because he was busy reading that, or was more profitably occupied than in reading either. Books are not much of a bugaboo in these days—there are too many of them. We look more and more to results and boggle less and less about processes. If so be the mind is alert and discriminating, and can choose what is good, and grasp it wherever he finds it, there is no vain questioning as to the particular books on which it gained its edge.

There is a good old saw about judging a man by the company he keeps, and as saws go it is pretty sound doctrine. Judge a man if you will by his companions, taking due notice as to how far he gives himself up to them, and how much they mean to him; for of course there are men and men, and some men catch the tone of their associates and others give tone to them. Books are companions to many of us men and women, but if you undertake to judge us by the books we read you will have occasion to use your best discretion. People take their books so differently. Some of us do not exercise our minds enough in our daily toil, and we like when we read to read books substantial enough to sharpen our faculties. Others of us come home with tired wits and want easy books that will rest and amuse us. Two people may read the same novel with equal pleasure, yet if one reads it after breakfast and the other after dinner, the fact that it amused them both does not tell the same story about the quality of their minds. If the book which you read when you are tired is strong enough food for my mind when its energies are fresh, it must mean that your mind and my mind lack a good deal of being mates.

And besides, there are people to whom it comes natural to read, and there are others, even in these days of newspapers and schools, to whom reading comes hard. I have seen, as most of us have, so many thoroughly worthless persons who were great readers, that when I meet a thoroughly worthy and intelligent person who doesn't read, it fills me with admiration and respect. I do meet such persons now and then. They are apt to be quick and accurate observers, good talkers, people of action. Of course they do read a little something every day, the newspaper if nothing more, but reading is not a necessity to them. They don't count on it as an amusement or depend upon it as an exercise of the mind. To the habitual reader, reading becomes as necessary as alcohol to the dram-drinker. It doesn't seem to make any violent amount of difference what he reads, but he must sit in a chair a certain length of time every day and rest his eyes and his mind on a printed page. You can no more judge such a person by the book-company he keeps than you can judge a lunatic by the qualities of his keepers. His reading is habit. It never turns to energy; never influences action. He sleeps better after it; that is all.

III

WORK AND THE YANKEE

WORK AND THE YANKEE

IT is rumored that ammonia has been trained to haul street-cars, and promises to prove strong, docile, and cheap, not afraid of the cars, and able to run up hill without getting out of breath. Even in a decade so prolific of tractorian movements as the present one, this is a development that is not to be sneezed at. I suppose it is another bit of Yankee enterprise.

The Yankee's antipathy to work has never yet been adequately appreciated. He takes to it so effectively that you might think him a Rollo sort of person who does it for his play. But not so. He is in a state of perpetual insurrection against the primal curse. He feels that he was born to sit on the fence and whittle in the sunshine, and he is against every apparent necessity that would compel him to forego the serene pleasures of a purely contemplative existence. He recognizes, to be sure, that work has got to be done. No one has a more vivid realization of that. But the consciousness of the need of getting things done does not impel him to take his coat off and do them, so much as to contrive some way of accomplishing ends without working. The crudest, simplest way of doing that is to get rich enough to hire labor. Accordingly, the Yankee does try to get rich, and does not try in vain. It is not that he loves money so much, and desires to possess it, as that he loves labor so little.

But to get rich is only an indirect way of beating the tyrant. The Yankee would rather abolish work than elude it. If he can get it done without human intervention at all, he likes that best; and if he cannot wholly eliminate human intervention, he wants to reduce it to its lowest possible limit. When he gets matters fixed so that the work is done with very little intermeddling, he is willing to sit by and supervise the process. He will pull a lever

Work and the Yankee

and turn a cock now and then without much complaint, if so be that he can ruminate and whittle between times. It is not that he is lazy. His name is a synonyme for energy and perseverance. But to make things work together for the automatic accomplishment of labor, and to sit by and see that they work right—that is the Yankee idea of the mission of man.

It is the right idea ; perhaps even the highest idea that there is on the subject. Omnipotence, according to the reverent conception of some of the wisest philosophers, is not so much the ability to do all things, as to compel a spontaneous performance of allotted duties by all creation. So it may fairly be argued that it is not the Yankee's perversity but the divine spark in him that is at the bottom of his desire to make nature toil while he looks on. Of the propensity toward contemplation he has no monopoly. The seers of all times have shared that. It has peopled monasteries and convents, and enthusiastic Buddhists have been used these many centuries to give up all their time to it. But it is the distinction of the Yankee, admirably illustrated in the case of Lincoln, to combine the contemplative disposition with an acute sense of responsibility for the proper conduct of affairs. He insists upon having time to think, but he also insists that the work shall go on while he is thinking. It would not suit him merely to sit under a bo-tree and concentrate his mind on his own corporeal centre, nor yet to vegetate in a monastery. That would seem to him an evasion of responsibility. What he does do is to build a machine that will do his work while he sits by and watches it.

I wonder sometimes that with his intermixture of the meditative and the practical he has not made greater progress in developing the possibilities of prayer. Prayer might be loosely defined as one method of getting some things done without actually doing them, and in that aspect of it it might be expected to appeal to the Yankee. No doubt it does appeal to him, but he seems to have made no greater progress with it than his predecessors on earth in other climes and ages. Considering how long prayer has been in use in the world and how much human energy it has engrossed, it seems a remarkable thing that there should continue to be such uncertainty about its effects. When a boy throws a ball over a wall, he cannot tell precisely where it is going to land, but he is sure it went over and that it will hit something. When a doctor gives medicine he cannot be certain of its effect until the patient has shown it, and he cannot always be sure then; nevertheless he knows the medicine was an actual force and that it did something, though other forces may have neutralized its action. But when a man of average sentiments prays he is not sure whether or not anything has gone out from him which has had any effect outside of his own range of perception. He is sure that his own mind has worked in a certain manner. If other persons have heard him pray, he may be convinced that his uttered sentiments have affected their minds, but beyond that everything is foggy and uncertain.

Some possibilities of prayer.

That is an unsatisfactory state of things,

with which prayerful persons ought not to be satisfied. If prayer is worth using at all, and great numbers of intelligent people are convinced that it is, it is worth using with the utmost intelligence and the highest attainable skill. The kind of prayer in which the petitioner asks for everything he can think of, in the hope that some of his supplications may reach the mark, is as much out of date as those doses affected by doctors of the last generation, in which a lot of drugs were mixed, not for their combined effect, but in the hope that the right one might be among them, and might find its way to the right spot in the patient. Perhaps clumsy doctors do that way still. Not so the masters of medicine. Their diagnoses make plain to them what they want to do; then, if they use a drug at all, it is sent to accomplish that particular purpose. So, in this enlightened generation, the prayers of the great prayer-masters should be rifle-shots sent by an understood force at an ascertained mark. Whether they hit or miss should depend upon comprehensible conditions. If a savage fires at the moon with a rifle, he may be surprised at not hitting it; but a man who understands about rifles is not surprised. He knows what may be expected of them. So it should be possible to understand prayer.

There are forces of nature which used to be mysterious, but which the men of our day can use and control, because they have learned how. If there are natural forces which can be reached or directed by prayer, it is not unimaginable that human intelligence may gain a more definite use, and some measure of control of them also. Men pray to God, but there is no natural force that the idea of God does not include. The more rational idea of prayer would seem to be not an argument or entreaty which influences the sentiments of the Deity, but a force which acts directly on some force which is included in God. Of prayer so considered it is as obvious a necessity that the results it seeks should accord with God's will as that the results expected from the control of other natural forces should accord with the laws of nature. Men do not expect water to run up hill and turn a mill-wheel. They have found out that water runs down hill. But if the use of water was still in the experimental stage they might put their mill-wheels at various points to see what results they got. Until they learned the laws of nature as they affect water, water-power would be a mysterious and uncertain force.

Prayer is still in the experimental stage. We know that it is of no use as a force, except so far as it conforms to the will of God. Yet many of us believe that it brings things to pass which would not happen without it. Electricity works in accordance with the will of God when it hauls a street car, but it would not haul the car except for the interposition of the will of man. So we constantly use prayer as though it were an objective force, subject to the will of man in accordance with the will of God. We are pretty sure that the will of God, including and regulating all natural forces, is invariable, not subject to whims or argument or entreaty. When we pray, then, we do not hope to alter God's will, but rather for the application to a special case of some force whose existence is suspected rather than understood, which is included, as are all natural forces, in God, but which, like other forces, is subject to our will in proportion as we understand the laws that govern it. But we don't seem to know enough about prayer yet to adapt our methods with any certainty to its possibilities. We set up our mill-wheels and wait to see which way the force tends, and whether or not it will turn them. We string our wires, but don't quite know how to get the electricity into them. We cannot gear our wants by prayer to the great central force so as to get our necessities satisfied. When we have more nearly perfected our knowledge of prayer, and of the will of God, we will, perhaps, be able to do that very thing. Then, when we see a comet coming our way we may be able to pray our planet out of its course as easily as we steer a ship out of the course of another and avoid a collision. Then, when we are in such a predicament as often are the passengers of a disabled steamer, we can count with some certainty upon calm seas and succor from the nearest ship.

Man is not the supreme force of the Universe, but he is akin to it. He shares its quality. All things are possible to him if only he can learn how. If he can ever become the reverent master of scientific prayer, we may expect to see the rate of his progress indefinitely accelerated. The incurable will be cured then; the impracticable will be done; the secret of perpetual motion will be revealed; the fountain of youth will gush out. The millennium will have come, but only for those who learn to know it.

IV

CHORES

CHORES

IT is complained of the times that they make too many specialists. The economical division of labor seems to demand that workers shall confine themselves to a particular detail of a job, which passes out of their hands to be completed. Editors no longer set type and write up local occurrences. Physicians, in increasing numbers, confine their ministrations to the eye, or the ear, or the throat, or the vermiform appendix. Among artisans it is the exception when a single tailor completes a coat, or one machinist makes a complete machine. Consequently specialists abound and all-around men are scarce.

Now, it is economical and profitable on various accounts to be a specialist, but there are charms, and even a measure of advantage, about being an all-around man, and means that tend to preserve the capacity to deal with things in general, without sacrificing the mastery of something in particular, are worth cultivating in the interest of general development. That must be the developing specialist's justification in cultivating the branch of domestic industry known as "chores." It is apparently wasteful for a man who can earn several dollars an hour at the work which is his specialty to spend any of his time in labor which can be better performed for him by the man whose time is worth very much less. If the better paid man lets his chores encroach upon the hours that belong to his special work, he certainly is wasteful, but it does not prove that it is wiser for him to forego chores altogether. In moderation and at proper times they are good for him. As a rule, the better he is paid for the hours he spends on his regular job, the fewer hours he works at it. That is not because he is satisfied with less than he can earn, but because high-priced work is usually exhausting, and cannot be long kept up without loss of quality. So the best-paid men commonly have some leisure, part of which they should devote to culture and various supplementary duties, and part, I maintain, to chores which cannot be left out without appreciable detriment.

We are used to being told that it is not enough to give mere money to charity, and that our benefactions, if they are to do the most good to us and to those whom they help, must include personal service. We seem to owe a measure of personal service to domestic life as well as to charity, and if we do not pay it, domestic life does not yield to us all that we might get out of it. The ability to do things depends partly upon our willingness to do them now and then. But the ability to do things is power, and power is very sweet to have and to exercise, and that not only in great things but in small. The man who cannot do the ordinary small tinkering that has to be done from week to week in an ordinary modern house denies himself a consciousness of power which is very cheap at the price it costs. Not to be able to put washers on a leaky water-faucet, to take off or put on gas-burners, and to remedy the simpler maladies of plumbing, is to admit one's self to be the mere occupant, but not the master, of the modern house. To put in glass takes too much time, and altogether it is not as necessary to the modern as it was to his grandfather that he should know how to be his own glazier. So with most carpenter work. It takes too long to do well any job of consequence; better have in the adept from his shop. And yet some tools and the ability to use them seem to be indispensable to the householder's self-respect. Not to be able to plane the top of a door or the edge of a drawer when it sticks; or to drive a nail straight, or send home a screw without splitting the wood, or fit a key, or mend a child's toy, must involve a humiliating consciousness of inefficiency. Yet there are men who strive to reconcile with self-esteem all these incompetencies, and another more inexcusable than either of them—the inability to run a furnace and raise or lower the temperature of one's habitation at will.

Chores

Tuning pianos and mending dormant clocks are accomplishments, and do not come under the head of ordinary chores. Moreover, they are occupations of elegant leisure, and not for the odd moments of a busy life. But with true chores it is different. There is a flavor about them which is too valuable to be lost out of life. A householder who has none that he recognizes might almost as well live in a hotel. He is the sort of man who rings for a servant when the fire falls down. Poor helpless one, who misses so much of the luxury of doing things for himself!

In my own case I recognize a possibility that I may shortly come to have leisure for all the self-improvement in the way of chores that I care to undertake, for since my brother Mundanus has become rich and famous as the author and autocrat of the Boot-Jack Trust, I have been very strongly tempted to stop working for myself and arrange with him for my support. It may be that I shall conclude that the habit of drudgery is too firmly fixed on me to be thrown off with impunity, so that

The profit and loss of having a famous brother.

perhaps I shall elect to go on working; but if I do, it will be in the nature of a self-indulgence, maintained for mere personal ease, against my conviction of what is just and right. For my argument is, and it is conceived on general and impersonal grounds, and founded without prejudice on dispassionate observation, that a comfortable maintenance without work is a very moderate set-off to any ordinary man for the inconvenience and detriment of having an immoderately successful brother. The reason lies in the incorrigible tendency of society to measure brothers by the same standard. When they are little, society puts them back to back and observes which is the taller. When they are grown, it piles their achievements or renown or incomes up side by side, and remarks which pile is bigger. Mr. Rockefeller's or Mr. Astor's income may run up into the millions, without making anyone think the worse of my capacity; but ever since it became known that Mundanus was getting fifty thousand a year (largely payable in Boot-Jack stock, as I happen to know, but the public doesn't)

Chores

it has been imputed to me as a fault, and somewhat of a disgrace, that my in-takings are not so large. It is so well understood as to be beyond argument or dispute, that in children of the same parents quite as much disparity of characteristics and abilities obtains as in persons who are not allied by blood. So also some brothers have a better education, or better opportunities, or better luck than others. Nevertheless, however conscientiously a man may have used the talents given him, and whatever honorable progress he may have made in life, if it be his misfortune to have a meteoric brother, who has sailed conspicuous where *he* has had to plod, and arrived glorious while *he* has sweated in patient aspiration, the slow-gaited man is bound to suffer as, I do, by disparaging comparison with his ocupod fellow of the same brood.

Lord Nelson had a brother, a clergyman, who might have passed down into a respectable obscurity but for a misfortune of birth which has lugged him into history as a person who, in spite of his breed, had no talent for fighting, and not even a reasonable regard for Lady Hamilton. William Nelson, however, at least inherited his brother Horatio's title and estates, and found in them, it is to be hoped, some compensation for the disparaging comparison from which he suffered. George Washington had a brother; but with the far-seeing consideration characteristic of a patriot-statesman, he buried him long before the Revolution. Lord Tennyson had a brother, who is best known to our time as that brother of the Laureate whose verse was not so good as Alfred's.

Analogous examples abound, some of them are so familiar that it would be indelicate to name them in print. What worthy and delightful men of our own day and nation have been overshadowed by the spreading renown of their brother, the great poet! What gifted and zealous preachers are best identified to-day as brothers of some supreme genius of the pulpit! There are some families, to be sure, as the Washburnes, the Adamses, the Shermans, the Fields, or the Potters, in which an inheritance of talent and energy has

Chores

been so evenly distributed that the whole brood seemed to climb abreast out of the ruck of common humanity. Such brothers as these are in a fortunate case, and the credit of each one helps up the others. But far more commonly it happens that when high success visits a family at all it comes in a lump upon a single member. How reasonable it would be in such cases if the less fortunate members should lament the success of the lucky one, and lay his renown up against him! To the credit of human nature be it noted that it seems usually not to happen that way. The remarkable law which decrees that he who has shall have more, usually proves its power, and the successful brother, besides the material advantages that his achievements bring him, commonly enjoys an exaggerated share of the esteem and admiration of his own kin. My brother Mundanus, by his notorious successes, has impaired my individuality. However hard I try, I can never hope hereafter to be known of men except as a brother of Mundanus of the Boot-Jack Trust. Yet I feel no resentment toward him. I rejoice in him, I am just as fond of him as ever, and proud of him besides. I make no effort to get out of his shadow. Our families still commune together, and it was only this morning that my eldest son suggested that my project of sending him to college was unwise, and that it would be vastly better for him to shelve his books and go down and strike his Uncle Mundanus for a job. I should prefer that Cato should go on with his studies, and shall so counsel him; but so far as his disposition to get something out of Mundanus is concerned, I am convinced that that is a sound instinct and based on equity.

V

CONSIDERATIONS MATRIMONIAL

CONSIDERATIONS MATRIMONIAL

COUSIN ANTHONY has been in to tell me of the betrothal of his son Ajax to a young woman of exceptionally voluminous financial prospects. My cousin is not himself a man of large means, and his children's fortunes are still to be made; nevertheless it was not with- *Marrying a rich girl* out an air of deprecation and symptoms of uneasiness that he told me what Ajax had done. He confided to me the name of the maiden's father, and little as I know about finance I recognized its fiscal potency, and realized the probability that the daughter of such a parent would some day be very rich. I asked Anthony how it happened. He could not tell me much. It had been sudden news to him, and wholly unexpected. Beyond the fact that it *had* happened he knew little. Ajax had asked neither his advice nor his consent. The young woman's natural protectors had apparently made no effort to interfere. If she chose to marry Ajax they seemed willing that she should do so, and the engagement was liable to be announced at any moment on the ticker-tapes, and in the society columns of the daily papers.

I congratulated Anthony, of course; but it was evident that the disparity between his son's fortune and that of his prospective daughter-in-law embarrassed him, and that he had come in not so much to be felicitated as to be reassured. So I did my best to reassure him.

Remarking (not without some private satisfaction in the thought) that Ajax seemed to feel entirely competent to manage his affairs, and that, anyhow, the business had already passed the point where interference was possible, I proceeded to dwell at some length on the disadvantages that had to be overcome by a young man of character and ability who married a very rich girl. What such a young man was after in life was of course to work out what was in him. As long as he was tolerably poor he had the stern incentive of scant means, and if a family became dependent on his efforts, the incentive became so much the stronger. In that case he must work hard, take care of his health, grasp every chance, be temperate, thrifty, and far-sighted, since only by the most earnest devotion could he hope for such success as would yield him the comforts of life. But to the husband of a woman of fortune this incentive would be almost wholly lost, though the mischief might in some degree be counterbalanced by the opportunities for very advantageous labor which a powerful family connection may often control.

I went on to point out some of the perils which beset the path of the working husband of a rich wife. He may get lazy and stop work. It will be easy for him to do so, since if anything happens to check his labors the strain will be immediately relaxed, and someone will stand ready to undertake any task he may choose to lay down. Instead of having his endurance

is a risky venture,

strengthened by moderate hardship, he will be pampered. If he needs a week's rest, he will be urged to take a month; if he needs a month, he will be advised to go abroad and spend the summer. He will probably be over-fed and very possibly he will develop gout. He will drink champagne when he should be drinking claret, and claret when he should not be drinking at all. He will be liable to be called upon to waste much time aboard yachts; he will be exposed to many perils from horses; he will be liable to travel at short notice to the remotest places for the benefit of his health, or his wife's health, or the health of his children; he must run the risk of being oppressed by a multiplicity of servants, and of having his energies frittered away in detail by the cares of large establishments. He will be nagged by promoters who will offer him opportunities to invest his wife's surplus income. It will be very hard for him to stick to business. Small matters will not be worth his attention, and the direction of large concerns is not to be learned without prelim-

Considerations Matrimonial

inary training in affairs of less importance. Then there will be his children. He will have to see that his boys are not ruined by luxury, and that adventurers do not steal his daughters.

But, of course, I went on to say, seeing Anthony growing solemn, somebody must marry the rich girls. There might be enough rich young men to pair off with them if all the rich bachelors were available; but as long as a large percentage of the rich bachelors insist on marrying poor girls there is no choice but for some rich girls to marry poor men or none. And, after all, if a girl is truly a nice girl, it would be a shame to avoid her because of her fortune. When I was young, I told him, if I had really loved a girl, and she had loved me, and had been of age or an orphan, I would have married her if she had owned all New York between Canal Street and Central Park. Dreadful as it would have been to be burdened with such a load I would have felt that a true affection might make it tolerable. *but not necessarily unprofitable.*

I think I was a comfort to cousin Anthony. He went away looking a good deal less dejected than when he came in. What a happiness it is, to be sure, when one gets a chance to benefit a fellow - creature's spirits by changing his point of view! I did no violence to my conscience either in speaking to him as I did, for really there is no insuperable objection to marrying a very rich woman and even living on her money. Most men prefer wives with incomes, all other things being equal, if they are to be had. It is true that prudent husbands prefer some measure of financial independence, and are loath to rest their entire maintenance on a wife's provision; but that is a matter of detail, and it is not necessarily discreditable to even an able-bodied man that he should live on his wife's money. If there is money enough it may be more convenient for both of them and all concerned that it should be used in that way. Good husbands are worth all rich women can afford to give.

It accords very definitely, however, with public opinion that dependent husbands of rich women should be good husbands.

Considerations Matrimonial

Rightly or wrongly, there is more patience with the failures of men who are casually married than with those with whom domestic life is a profession. If the dependent husband of a rich wife earns his maintenance no man is better entitled to the respect of the community. If he can keep his wife's respect, cultivate her intelligence, keep her mind in a progressive state, and make her reasonably happy and do equally well by himself, he is performing a difficult part in a creditable and workman-like manner, and has no occasion to fret about where his money comes from. He cannot justly be held answerable for results, because his most conscientious efforts may not be successful. If he cannot make his wife affirmatively happy he should try to keep her from becoming aggressively discontented, and even though he fails in that, he should still endeavor to keep her respectable. If he ceases to be her lover, he should still be her protector. Married or otherwise, it is an achievement to be respectable and a considerable feat to maintain a tolerable continuity of happiness.

I was saying the other day to that stately lady, Mrs. Damocles, that I had such a high opinion of Winship, partly because of his exceptionally enlivening personal qualities and partly for his marvellous discrimination in the choice of a wife. And I added that I had the very highest opinion of Mrs. Winship because of her sense and her loveliness, and especially because of her success in living with Winship and being his wife. Now Winship is a good man and delightful company. He is pretty to look at and very good indeed to go; but he has a prodigious enjoyment of life and such an unbroken eagerness to taste everything that is good, and be in everything that is moving, that I felt that I cast no reflection upon him when I said that for a woman to live with him, as Mrs. Winship did, was a great feat.

"It is a great feat," remarked Mrs. Damocles, with a certain air of giving her mind relief, "for any woman to live with any man, or any man to live with any woman."

"Well, if it comes to that," said I, "I presume it is, and it is a feat exceedingly

Considerations Matrimonial

well worth accomplishing. I find I have more and more respect the older I grow for people who hit it off gracefully and successfully."

That was true. I do have such a sentiment for such people, and I dare say it is a sentiment as common as it is well founded. It is a considerable feat for a grown man and a grown woman to live together happily, and the people who accomplish it in any high degree of perfection must either be very nice people or must try very hard. I respect them either way, whether their success is due to natural sweetness or to sustained effort. People who are capable of sustained effort to maintain the harmony of their domestic relations are very good sort of people. They must have fidelity, that king-pin among the virtues, and divers other strong ingredients that go to make up what we call "good stuff." I am not sure but that we should respect them even more than folks who are simply born sweet and reasonable, and who love each other and get on without trying.

The happily married

It is matter of record that in patriarchal and scriptural times it was held a thing particularly good and pleasant to behold brethren dwell together in unity. That man and wife should dwell in that way seems not to have been thought so affecting a spectacle. Perhaps it was held that if a patriarch could not live harmoniously with one wife, he could with another, or perhaps the sentiment of the times favored hammering a disorderly wife with a tent-pin until she became tractable, so that domestic tranquillity was taken for granted. It is not surprising that with changed conditions and the new woman we moderns should have assumed a different point of view. Where we look on it is pleasant to be sure to see brethren brotherly, but it is no great matter if they differ, for the world is big enough for them all. But the world is not big enough for the successful disagreement of man and wife. They may part, but it is not success; it is failure. Both must carry away the marks of it, and whatever may happen neither is quite as good as before. In spite of divorce laws and all easements of that sort, we have contrived to make a deeply serious business of marriage. We ought to applaud those who succeed in it, because success is so indispensably necessary.

It would be a little different if folks were really free to marry or not as they chose, with no fierce bugaboo behind the alternative. But the fact is the majority of us are not quite free, for there is a bugaboo behind. We are taught and believe that, if we don't marry, a worse thing may happen to us, for we will grow old without either the discipline or the companionship of a mate, without children to bring youth back into our lives; indeed, without the elements of a home. We see people in this predicament, and though there are plenty of encouraging exceptions, on the whole celibacy seems so very second-rate to most of us that we don't bargain for it except under stress of strong necessity. Marriage in most cases seems so preponderately expedient that we would feel that we ought to marry even if we didn't want to, and as

and their claim

usually we do want to, marriage becomes, practically, a necessity.

I declare that I am personally grateful to married people who get on conspicuously well. They are a reassuring spectacle in society, and as part of society I take comfort in knowing them, and am obliged to them for existing. And, of course, I am especially obliged to the women like Winship's wife, who are particularly good wives. You should see that lady, how she holds that hare-brained creature, not with too tight a lariat or too loose; neither nagging nor neglectful; not so dependent on him as to shackle him, nor so independent as to leave him too free. Of course, she couldn't do it it unless she was a woman of brains, and unless Winship was a good fellow—a fellow, that is, with some gaps in his selfishness. She is too good a wife for him, but I am glad he has got her, and so, unmistakably, is he.

The most effectual argument in favor of marriage is the average bachelor of forty-five. That is as it should be. There are bachelors of mature years who are of such

to our applause.

use to society as to justify their condition, but the average old bachelor is a warning, as he ought to be. He is a shirk, and I have not much patience with him. For the average spinster I have much more respect. Her habits are almost always a great deal better than the bachelor's, and she commonly differs from him in being able, not only to take care of herself, but of other people. Provided she does not exist in excessive numbers, her existence is rather an advantage than a detriment to her fellows. I like to see her get everything that ought to be coming to her, including her full share of liberty, and as much happiness as she is able to divert to her own use. It is a question how far liberty is conducive to happiness, but if the ratio between the two is direct, the contemporary American spinster ought to be happier than spinsters have ever been in time past, for never spinster had her own way to the same extent as she. In a discourse about middle age, contributed some time ago to the *North American Review*, Mrs. Kate Gannett Wells said : " Middle life for an unmarried daughter is often very hard, for she may have no real liberty. A girl at forty ought to have her own choices just as much as if she were married."

For a woman writer, a married woman writer, to say "her own choices just as much as if she were married," is an impressive bit of unsolicited testimony to the freedom of married women in America, and their habit of doing just as they please. It is true, moreover, that unmarried daughters of reasonably mature years should have just as much freedom as their characters and circumstances will permit. If they are not to have the natural career that is desired for womankind, they should be free to make some other kind of career for themselves, if they are able.

The contemporary spinster,
It is an exceptional married woman who will find it possible to "have her own choices" in anything like the same degree as the coming spinster of forty, who finds herself released from parental constraint and free to get out of the world as much as she can. The earth is to be hers and the fulness thereof. It is opening to her, and

Considerations Matrimonial

she is advancing upon it with flying feet. She promises to be one of the freest of mortal creatures, and one of the most coercive and competent. Clubs are growing up in great cities for her convenience; big buildings are planned for her to live in; charities are looking to her for management; dependent relatives are to owe their support to the results of her intelligent exertions. There was a time when the ideal condition coveted by women who craved unlimited freedom was that of a widow with one child. Widowhood grows yearly less necessary, and though the single child is as desirable as ever, it is because a child is a pleasure, and not because one is needed as a protection. There is very little left in the way of the spinster who has enlightened parents, and the enlightenment of parents is making such progress that in the course of another generation we may expect to see it customary to provide for the inclination of unmarried women for an independent existence.

The independence of married women is secured by law, and is definitely ascertained.

her privileges and

The independence of unmarried women of mature years, which naturally follows and was bound to follow, depends not on statutory enactment, but on social custom and notions of propriety. Of course it takes longer to change the views of proper people upon propriety than it does to make a new statute; but the change is coming. How many spinsters does each of us know who have summer cottages on their own hook, where, for part of the year at least, they are a law unto themselves? How many who support themselves? How many who travel where they will without any other than financial limitations? There is a good deal of solace for the spinster in these days, and there is abundant reason to be glad of it.

The spinster is a great boon to individuals, though perhaps the State has good reasons for not approving of her. Likewise to families. In a land where men have little leisure to visit, and where the habits of married women and children are influenced, if not absolutely regulated, by the habits of men, the spinster can make

her great usefulness.

visits, thereby keeping up old friendships and bringing new atmospheres into homes that have need of wholesome variation. The spinsters form the nearest approach to a leisure class in America. A vast work is done by them all the time. A vaster work awaits them. All social philosophers who know anything will hail with approval all indications that promise increased liberty and thereby increased usefulness to spinsters.

VI

LOVE, FRIENDSHIP, AND GOSSIP

LOVE, FRIENDSHIP, AND GOSSIP

COUSIN ANTHONY tells me that he has been taken regularly to task by two dames of his acquaintance because he does not dwell oftener in his literary deliverances upon the incident of love. Love, they told him—and he said they were both matrons who had lived long enough in the world to know — was the best thing in life, and there was nothing that people liked better to read about. They insisted that it was a professional blunder on his part not to write love-stories and not to work more of the tender passion into his business generally. Anthony said that he promised to amend, but he admitted that he had small hopes of doing so, for he never had been able to make love-literature, and it was late in life for him to

Love in books.

begin. He insisted that the love that was of real value in the world wasn't interesting, and that the love that was interesting wasn't always admirable. Love that happened to a person like the measles or fits, and was really no particular credit to itself or its victims, was the sort that got most into books and was made much of; whereas the kind that was attained to by the endeavor of true souls, and that had wear in it, and that made things go right instead of tangling them up, was too much like duty to make satisfactory reading for people of sentiment. If he ever did write a love-story he believed he would have no women in it at all, unless, possibly, just one to make the necessary trouble. Not but that women did their full share of all the loving that was done, and did it to admiration, but because to portray a man's love for a man would give the sentiment of love, he thought, in its simplest and most lucid form, uncomplicated by the incident of sex. When a man loved a man you knew what you had; but when he was in love with a woman the diagnosis was full of perplexities, and how much of his seizure was passion, how much hysteria, and how much sincere affection, were subtleties too fine for mere laymen to struggle with.

I do not think that Anthony will ever write acceptably on love, and it is probably a wise instinct that steers him clear of that department of literature. Indeed, I do not think he fully understands the subject. And yet there is something to be said for his suggestion that the more admirable species of love and the worthiest to dwell upon, is not that which one falls into willy-nilly, but which is resolutely given out of the heart. The love into which volition enters is true love, quite as genuine as the involuntary emotion which figures in love at first sight. Faithfulness is surely about the best quality that love can possess, and the very idea of faithfulness implies volition. The popular mind recognizes the element of volition in love. It expects people to love persons whom they ought to love or whom they have undertaken to love. If a man has a lovable wife and does not love her, it does not pity him as an unfortunate; it blames him as a poor stick. It is right. If the man is in love with his wife, he is in luck to be sure, and he ought to be thankful; but if not, it is no excuse for his not loving her. He ought to be able to love her if he chooses, and if she will let him he ought to choose. That is the *vox populi* in the matter, but perhaps in this case it is not divine, for certainly the love-story writers are not out of breath with trying to echo it. They are almost too prone to treat the master-passion as a wind that bloweth where it listeth and nowhere else, and some of them have even been known to coddle married persons in their stories who run up against extra-parietal affinities and are wrecked in the resulting tumult. But, of course, the exigencies of story-making are imperative, and the demand for stories with love in them being urgent and steady, the people who supply it must be suffered to write them as they can, even though it may revolt some thrifty souls to see misery misbuilt out of the materials of happiness.

Platonic love seems not to be of much use

to the story-makers unless it is always on the verge of some unplatonic excess. Perhaps it is due to the artificers of romance and their disparagement of it as a thing not useful to them in their business that our opinion of its instability is so decided. Of course they are not all against it. One of them, Sir Walter Besant, has been discussing platonic friendships, and whether or not they can really be made to work. He thinks they may, but not between two persons both of whom are young.

It is well that someone should take thought about platonic friendships, for Nature, who superintends most things, does not seem to care very much about them. It makes no difference to her, apparently. whether they work or not. No great natural law governs them. The principle of natural selection shirks responsibility for them, and no one dares to assume that the fittest of them will survive. They cannot be left to take care of themselves, but, if they exist at all, must be constantly under supervision, and subjects of argument and special pleas.

Platonic friendships

Consider what the essentials of a platonic friendship are! Are they not that the parties to it shall be of different sexes, and that there shall be a considerable degree of exclusiveness about their intimacy? Does anyone doubt that exclusiveness is essential? Intimacy cannot be intimacy unless it is more or less exclusive. We can only live one life at a time, and if we share a good part of that with any one person, there is so much the less for the rest. If a friendship is not intimate enough to be noticeably exclusive, does anyone ever find it necessary to explain that it is platonic?

Love between women and men was not invented for the entertainment of philosophers, but largely for domestic purposes; and if platonic love is to have anything better than a hazardous and unstable existence, the conditions of it must be such that it may prosper without conflict with Nature's more important ends. Thus we see why platonic friendships between young people who might marry do not endure. Such couples get married, and their friend-

Love, Friendship, and Gossip

ship merges into a more durable sentiment, or else one of them marries someone else, and then it lapses. At least it should lapse, for if it does not, it not only militates against peace in a family, but it tends to keep the unmarried platonist from going about his business and finding himself a mate, according to Nature's design. It is true that there are women, and young women at that, who can contrive for a time to maintain a husband and a simultaneous platonic intimate. But in such cases one of three things happens: either the wife makes her husband happy and her platonic admirer miserable, or she makes her friend happy and her husband miserable, or she makes them both miserable. If by any chance or miracle of talent she seems to make them both happy, she makes society miserable, because it cannot see how she does it. And when society is miserable it talks; until finally it breaks up the arrangement. She is bound to fail, and the reason does not lie in any defect in her, but in the fact that her purpose is contrary to the economy of Nature, which

and their drawbacks.

has provided barely men enough to go around, and does not permit a woman who has a man of her own to monopolize other men with impunity. Every marriageable man besides her husband that any woman absorbs involves the waste of some other woman's opportunities, and Nature abhors waste with a proverbial antipathy.

As for the platonic friendships of young married men, they are hardly worth discussing. The measure of them is simply the wife's capacity to control her feelings. It becomes clear, therefore, that the only platonic friendships that can be trusted are those that do not interfere with Nature's plans. Young lads, " hobbledehoys," if they are not too rich, may cultivate with impunity transitory friendships with women somewhat older than themselves. Such associations are instructive to the lad and amuse the lady, without interfering in any way with her more serious plans. So also there are adult men, who, by reason of special circumstances or exceptional personal qualities, gain special privileges of platonic attachment. It is part of the record of the Chevalier Bayard that he loved dearly and without concealment another gentleman's wife, but he was irreproachable and was not a marrying man, and what was even more important, he was almost always absent on warlike adventures, so that no one grudged him the occasional solace he found in the lady's society. A considerable measure of platonic affection can be tolerated in almost any case, if it is only tempered by an adequate provision of absence.

Society's weapon, as I have said, against an excess of platonic friendship is talk. It is the sort of talk known as gossip. It is rather an ugly weapon at the best, and there is always more or less doubt among kind and conscientious people as to whether its use is justifiable or is a mere indulgence of their baser dispositions. What does the present reader think about it herself? Is there a justification for it? Does it serve any purpose useful enough to warrant its existence? Does a person who refuses to take part in it show himself superior to his fellows, or does he shirk an obligation that he owes to society? When Jack Harebrain's attentions to young Mrs. McFliget become audaciously conspicuous, and the whole community sits around and discusses them, is the community engaged in a valuable work that demands to be done, or is it merely giving evidence of its malicious disposition and the emptiness of its mind?

Excuses for gossip.

There are offences against society which it is the duty of the district-attorney, when he learns of them, to bring to the notice of the grand jury, to the end that their perpetrator may account to the law for his actions. There are also doings which society regards as offensive to itself of which the district-attorney can take no notice, and which are not of sufficient turpitude to engage the grand jury's attention. But in every household there are self-constituted grand jurors who sit on malfeasances of this sort when the gossips bring the news of them. Yet the gossips, instead of being commended for their vigilance, are pretty generally execrated, and most of us, when we share their labors, do it at some cost to our own self-respect, and very likely execrate ourselves.

Now, it is possible that in the loftiness of our conceptions we condemn ourselves overmuch, and restrain a propensity that has been cultivated in us for good. Gossip that pries into hidden proceedings, that suggests worse motives than appear, that carries tales and makes defamatory suggestions, is one thing. Gossip that discusses facts that are patent is another. If we should see Jake Hardman running away with Charles McFliget's pocket-book we should think ill of ourselves if we did not cry "Stop thief!" and join in the chase after the rascal. But suppose we think we see Jack Harebrain in the act of robbing McFliget of the affections of his wife. Are we really entitled to think better of ourselves for holding our tongues and overlooking this apparent larceny, than if we expressed our sentiments freely one to another? If there is enough talk, Flora McFliget's ears will be close stopped indeed if some of it does not find its way into them. Is it a kindness to her or to

Jack to let their behavior pass unnoticed? When there is a bridge down on the railroad and a train is coming, it may be disconcerting to the engineer to halloo and wave a red flag at him, but after all it is kinder to jar his nerves a little while there is still time to pull up, than out of an extreme politeness to let him go to destruction.

Besides, have we not ourselves and our own morals to consider, and how it may affect our own standards of behavior, to look on without remonstrance at such doings as Jack's and Flora's? If we ignore that sort of impropriety when it is done in plain sight, we may come presently to think there is nothing amiss in it, and even to take a turn at it ourselves.

It seems possible that because gossip is disagreeable it does not get even the moderate amount of credit that is its due. It is conceded to be lively talk, but it is felt to be unamiable, and even mean. But if it were wholly bad, decent people of strong convictions about right and wrong would not countenance it, whereas such people do at times countenance and even take part in it, and not without occasional good results.

People do not abstain from crimes for fear of being talked about, but they do oftentimes check themselves in indiscretions out of regard for us gossips, and what we may say about them. Newspapers take pretty complete charge of society nowadays, and with some slight help from the courts see that human conduct is regulated before it gets intolerable. But the newspapers cannot take cognizance of everything, and some things which they are compelled to overlook it may be our province as gossips to see to. If Jack Harebrain and Mrs. McFliget actually elope, the newspapers will attend to their case down to its remotest details; but so long as their dispositions are susceptible of cure, a worse thing may happen than for the gossip's court to take note of their case and try to laugh them back to good behavior.

VII

WOMAN SUFFRAGE

WOMAN SUFFRAGE

Y son Nicodemus is a tractable little boy and pleasant company. I like to have him along when I take my walks abroad, and he likes to go. But of late his mother has devised objections and insinuated impediments when I have wished him to accompany me, and several times I have found myself shuffling reluctantly off without him, and yet without any tangible reason for leaving him behind. But I have since discovered the reason, which is, that his mother sees so much fault found with man in the current newspapers and magazines that she fears its effect upon my impressionable nature, and has forebodings of a day when I shall come home alone, and tell her that I have felt compelled, on humanitarian grounds, to drop little Nicodemus into the river.

The current disparagement of man.

I trust her misgivings are not well-founded, but I cannot blame her for entertaining them; for certainly, if we are to believe Madame Sarah Grand and some other prophets of the magazines, to raise a man-child in these days is to do humanity something very like a grievous wrong. "What is man," exclaims the Psalmist, "that thou art mindful of him!" Madame Grand and her sisters could have told him. Man, as they are mindful of him, is an unlucky after-thought of the Creator, who, for lack of discipline and due subjection, has developed into a gross being drunken with a sense of his own importance, the oppressor of womankind, the blot upon Nature's face that messes her perfections.

There is no use in pretending to question the accuracy of this description, or in denying that there would be no trouble in the world worth mentioning if it were not for man. He is a poor creature, and always has been; and ever since the human experiment began it has been one long uphill struggle to try to make a good thing out of him, and make him do right. No sane person has ever blamed woman for man's shortcomings. In spite of the story of Eve and the serpent, man has had to bear the blame for himself, and so far as there was any blame to bear on woman's account he has had to stagger under that too.

That has been because he has been regarded as the stronger and more sensible of the two, and justly responsible for the condition of the human family. But there is a new theory now, set forth in serious books, and based on statistics and researches and scientific analogies, that woman is the better creature, and the one that knows more and is the better worth rearing. If this theory is correct, it involves a certain shifting of responsibility which the critics of man ought to recognize.

If woman is more of a man than man is, it is she who is to blame for his degradation, and not he for hers. She should never have permitted him to sink into those unutterable depths in which she sees him now. During all these years in which she has had him, she should have managed to hoist him up on to a decent plane, and make a respectable creature of him. If, on the other hand, he is a superior creature, the lord of creation, and responsible for his guilty self and for the woman besides, he should have due credit for what he has done well, as well as blame for his misdemeanors. It is notorious that the present progressiveness of women is unparalleled in human history. Shall he have no share of praise for that? If some women have climbed down on the ladder he has held, is no account to be taken of the multitude who have climbed up? Is it to be no mitigation of the discipline which he has maintained in the human family that womankind has thrived so amazingly under it?

Man, the poor old thing, is not getting justice. If he has governed the world all these years, the immense advance of women under his rule does him credit. But if he doesn't govern it, and never has been fit to govern it, woman ought to be ashamed to have neglected him as she has. For, according to the latest theories, he is simply what she has permitted him to become.

I have talked with Cousin Anthony

about Man, and also about Woman. He tells me that if woman suffrage comes to a vote in New York State he expects to vote against it. Such, he says, are the instructions that Mrs. Anthony has given him, and as his vote in the matter concerns her more than himself, he thinks himself even more than usually bound to execute her wishes. I found him quite fixed in the opinion — Mrs. Anthony's opinion — that the suffrage would do the New York women no good. The favorite representation of the reformers, that everyone is allowed to vote except aliens, minors, idiots, and women, seemed to have had no effect on Mrs. Anthony. She had no sort of doubt, of course (nobody has), that wise women were better qualified to vote than foolish men. She would not argue at all whether women were inferior to men or not. She could not see its bearing on the case. Her point of view was familiar enough, being simply that the suffrage was not a privilege but an obligation, and one which it did not seem to her the duty of our women at this time to assume. If the obligation to

Mrs. Anthony's displeasure with woman suffrage.

vote were laid with any discrimination upon individuals who had proved their capacity to exercise it, Mrs. Anthony thought the case would be different. She would not shrink from a duty that society by any reasonable process of selection seemed to have chosen her to bear. But when all the men could vote it was certainly no special honor to women to let all the women vote too. Nature had suggested in a large way the division of labor between men and women, and though the details of assignment varied from age to age, and Mrs. Anthony hoped that she was well up to the times in her estimate of the contemporary dimensions of woman's sphere, she did still believe in the division of labor, and she had not been able to learn of any mitigation of women's present duties by which it was proposed to offset the new task which threatened her. Mrs. Anthony declared, my cousin said, that so far as she understood her business in life she tried hard to do it. What she undertook she tried to undertake with her eyes open and with a definite intention of performing it as well as she could. If she was called to help manage a public charity and found herself able to respond, she went to the meetings of her colleagues and took her duties seriously. If children were born to her she tried industriously to raise them, to keep them clothed and healthy, and to bring them up, as far as she could, to be tolerably wise and good people. With her children, and her household, and her social duties, and her labors in the charities with which she was connected, Mrs. Anthony declared that her hands and her mind were full, and that the proposal to compel her to keep up with politics, to go to primaries and vote intelligently at elections was an imposition against which she rebelled. Men were willing enough nowadays to do for women almost anything that women really wanted done. They were particularly willing to let women do new kinds of work, especially ill-paid, vexatious work which they were inclined to shirk themselves. But what women really wanted was not so much the privilege of doing the men's work for them as to have the men do their own work and do it properly. There was nothing which women could gain by having the suffrage which they could not gain at far less expense by having men vote conscientiously. If there was fighting which it was indispensable to have done, Mrs. Anthony declared that she did not aspire to do it herself. She wanted her men to do it for her. She wanted her men to do her voting also. She demanded protection, security, and a reasonable amount of peace for the better furtherance of her duties already in hand, which were far too important and too engrossing to share her attention with practical politics. The suffrage once imposed upon women, they could never get quit of it, and it would be imposed, she feared, unless the mass of women, who don't want it and feel no obligation to undertake it, speak their minds and proclaim how they feel about it and why. Such, Anthony said, were his wife's sentiments. They are emphatic enough, certainly, and justify his intentions about his vote. How widely they are shared by intelligent women in New York State is hard to find out, because most of the women who think they want to vote sign petitions, and most of the women who don't, do nothing. But the particular thing that voting men in New York will want to know before they pass upon the woman suffrage question at the polls is, how large a proportion of the intelligent women in the State feel as Mrs. Anthony does, and prefer to have their voting done by their representative males.

It is remarkable with what unanimity, in appearance at least, the question has been left to women to settle. In all the talk about it there has been scarcely any inquiry as to whether it would cost men anything to give women the right to vote. The whole discussion has turned upon the probable effect of the ballot upon women, and has prevailed almost exclusively between those who have held that it would pay her to have a vote and those who have held that it would not. However men in general may have pondered in their secret hearts, they have had almost nothing to say as to whether it would pay them to *let* women vote. Representatives of some few special

Cousin Anthony and I

interests have had convictions about it, and have allowed them to come out. The liquor-dealers, for example, are generally understood to feel that woman-suffrage would be detrimental to their business interests; but they are alone among merchants, so far as I have noticed, in admitting that they could not afford to meet women at the polls. The milliners are not concerned as milliners; they do not fear that suffrage will affect the feminine taste in bonnets. The dry-goods men show no uneasiness. The manufacturers of infants' foods neither fear nor hope. Makers of bicycles are not especially hot for suffrage, nor are side-saddle manufacturers especially opposed to it. The average New York man does not seem to feel that anything unprecedented will happen whether woman-suffrage comes or not. It does not appear that he apprehends that his vote will be worth any the less to him because he shares it with a woman, or that his liberties will be restricted, or that the woman will be any less a woman because she shares his vote. Outwardly at least he has posed as

Bland demeanor of New York males towards the suffragists.

a spectator, interested indeed, but bland, courteous, and sympathetic even in his doubts. His behavior has been a credit to him. He has shown scarcely a sign of disposition to admit the existence or possibility of any antagonism between the interests of women and of men. He has not been over-ready to believe that it would be advantageous to women to vote, but his attitude has been that if it would be advantageous to them he will not stand in their way; and while he has not bound himself to accept their opinion as to the benefits of suffrage he has certainly shown an unaffected desire to know what their opinion is, and decided symptoms of a willingness to be guided by it.

Appearances are not absolutely to be trusted, but so far as they may guide one's judgment, man in New York really does not care very much, so far as he himself is concerned, whether woman votes or not. Certainly his attitude is admirable. It is intelligent and affectionate and respectful; and yet man never assumed an attitude that showed more conclusively his confidence in the authenticity of his commission as Lord of Creation. Even those exceptionally vehement suffragists who denounce him as the Tyrant do not scare him. He is not dismayed at any possible hosts of skirted voters that those ladies may array against him. He knows that the ballot is but an instrument and the voters are but the keys, and he seems content that whoever can shall play what tune they may. The possibility of more keys does not worry him, though he has not yet conceded its advisability, for he knows that be they many or few, they will all yield their most effectual music to the hands that are best adapted to touch them. The tune, man thinks, will be about the same as heretofore, and there will be no sweeping shiftings of performers; but if more notes will give fuller or more harmonious music, for his part he seems ready to have them.

Such, and so confident, is his attitude. The only wonder is that it has not occurred to any observant woman to satirize it in a gentle essay on "A Certain Condescension in Males."

VIII

THE KNOWLEDGE OF GOOD AND EVIL

THE KNOWLEDGE OF GOOD AND EVIL

IT is prodigious what an amount of energy is sunk in the unsuccessful exercise of that inalienable right, the pursuit of happiness. One reason for the waste is that people are governed too much by the opinions of others as to what is pleasure, and neglect to get information that would fit them by analyzing their own experiences. Thousands and tens of thousands of people do things day after day with the purpose of enjoyment, which they never have enjoyed, and never will, but which they have learned to regard as intrinsically pleasant. They ride horses, they drive, hunt, dress, dance, or whatever it is, not because they get personal enjoyment out of those occupations, but because other people have enjoyed them.

Of course, happiness is a state of mind; and it is the mind, or the soul, that we want to get at. We know this well enough theoretically, but fail to act with reasonable intelligence upon our knowledge. To a certain extent, the mind is dependent for its states upon the conditions of the body, and we are rightly taught that a degree of attention must be paid to physical means if we are to get intellectual or spiritual results. But even with the enjoyment of a healthy body a very important share of the pleasure is quasi-intellectual. When he has well eaten or well drunken a man feels pleasantly disposed toward the world. His feelings warm, his sympathies are aroused, and he is happy in consequence.

The exhilaration of the racer or the huntsman, of the oarsman or the football player, any high degree of muscular activity in a healthy man, is perhaps the nearest to a purely physical pleasure; but even here it is a higher enjoyment when it is competitive activity, for competition itself is a notable and legitimate delight. "Rejoiceth as a strong man to run a race," the Scripture saith, and knows its business as usual; for trying to win involves a chance to lose, and that there is not much fun where there is not some hazard has been the rule since Eve acquired knowledge of evil at the same bite with good.

Of those purely intellectual joys that are analogous to the physical joys, not all are healthy. It is fun to develop and exercise the mind, just as it is to exercise the muscles; but there are joys of the intellectual glutton and the intellectual sot, joys that are not nearly as disreputable as they ought to be. Minds are clogged with over-feeding and racked by over-stimulation, just as stomachs are. The joys of acquisition are not to be despised. Making money is mighty pleasant; to have things is an unquestionable source of satisfaction; to collect rare commodities, orchids, race-horses, railroad-bonds is a kind of sport that thousands of people follow with lively enthusiasm. It is fun to have and to hold, to add to and complete, and it has been since who knows how many centuries before Ahab longed for Naboth's vineyard. But avarice in all its forms, old-fashioned and venerable as it is, is only a second-rate sport, since it lacks the element that the greatest pleasures must have, the element of love.

Not passion. Passion is one of your second-rate, quasi-physical pleasures, which are half pain, and cannot be depended upon. But love is quite a different matter, and so detached from all that is bodily about us, as to breed the hope that it will still be a pleasure to us when we have taken our bodies off. When we have loved the most, and with the least passion and the least selfishness, was it not then that we attained most nearly to the state of mind which is the great prize of life?

We cultivate the muscles because it is fun to use them, and because it brings us the happiness that comes of health. For like reasons we make a business of the cultivation of our minds. How simple it is of us to neglect to the extent that most of us do the systematic cultivation of our hearts! Now and then someone discovers that to love one's neighbor with enthusiasm is the best fun there is, and makes a business of

The Knowledge of Good and Evil

doing it; and then the rest of us lean on our muck-rakes and gape at him, and wonder how he can spare so much time for such an object.

Analogous to the frequent inability of the human mind to recognize the attractiveness of what is really pleasant is the inaccuracy of its estimate of the repulsiveness of what is bad. It was said the other day of a man noted for his charitable estimate of his fellow-creatures that he would find something to admire in Satan himself. The remark was told him, and he said, "Yes, I always did admire the devil for his persistence." If he adopted the popular notion of Satan he might have found easily enough other grounds for admiring him; for while it is commonly held that the devil is not so black as he is painted, the better opinion seems to me to be that nowadays he is not painted anything like so black as he is, and that owing to the unfaithfulness with which his likeness is set forth he is very much more generally admired and respected than his qualities and

The current estimate of Satan.

true character deserve. The popular contemporary conception of Satan is of a highly successful man of the world. It is admitted that there are shady spots in his past history, that he has done some things that he should regret, that he is a hazardous associate and an unsafe person to have transactions with. But conversely it is realized that he is rich, powerful, and attractive, and intimately concerned and interested in promoting the material prosperity of the human race. He is known to be full of enterprise and public spirit, disposed to make things pleasant, and powerful in carrying the enterprises with which he is concerned to a profitable issue. It is true that he is understood to be unscrupulous, but it is felt that success excuses very much, and that when an individual has attained a position which enables him to be useful to the public it is a mistake to be over-nice about rejecting his good offices because in early life, when his necessities were more pressing, his methods or affiliations were not always such as a conscientious person could approve. Then, thanks to the mis-

The Knowledge of Good and Evil

directed zeal of a multitude of worthy persons who assume to abhor Satan and all his works, he gets credit for a host of things with which he really had very little to do. Lots of clergymen and others are sure that he invented all kinds of dances and laid the corner-stones of all the theatres. He gets immense credit all the time in certain quarters as the loosener of restrictions as to the use of the Sabbath, so that in some parts of the country folks can hardly walk in the fields on a Sunday afternoon without a sense of obligation to him for his share in the enlargement of their liberties. Inasmuch as he is earnestly and continuously denounced by hordes of good and zealous people as the discoverer and promoter of all exhilarating beverages, people who like beverages of that sort and feel safe in consuming them in moderate quantities cannot help a certain kindliness of feeling toward him on that account.

The upshot of all this perversion is that the enemies of the Adversary have unwittingly carved him out a great reputation as the champion of personal liberty, and the purveyor of manifold terrestrial delights which are not necessarily hurtful to those who realize them with discretion, and which are undeniably in favor with the natural man. Consequently it is easy for him to masquerade as a public benefactor, and folks, without admitting even to themselves how well they think of him, grow to feel that perhaps he has come to be good-natured in his old age, and that, nowadays, anyhow, his behavior seems pretty square, and that, maybe, the stories of his depravity do him an injustice.

To give the devil his due is proverbially proper, but to make such a hero of him is not only inexpedient but very bad morals. John Milton is partly to blame for it, for he first made Satan grand and semi-respectable, but the work has made great progress since his day. The pleasantest and most reassuring line in the prayer-book is that which describes the service of God as perfect freedom. If that idea of God's service could be more generally disseminated, with due supplementary inculcation of the truth that all the salutary and truly pleasant things in life are the gifts of God, and not devices of the Evil One, Satan would come much nearer to getting his due than he usually does come nowadays, or is likely to come perhaps until the final reckoning.

My young friend McAllo seems to be a victim of this familiar confusion of ideas as to what constitutes freedom and what does not. The last time he dined at our house, he shocked me a good deal by declaring that the chief object of his activities for some time past had been to rid himself of the weight of "Puritanism" which he had incurred from several generations of straight-laced ancestors. I inquired of McAllo what his descent was, and discovered that it was almost purely Scotch Presbyterian, and that what small admixture of other stock there was, was French Huguenot. McAllo complained that such a derivation as that was a hindrance to sport, and admitted that he had been busy for months past with horses, cocktails, cigarettes, and most of the reasonable appliances of generous living, trying to modify the

McAllo's impatience of his Puritanism.

tendencies that his forebears had imposed upon him. His conscience, he said, was too exacting, and he felt it to be desirable to mitigate its tyranny.

I was affected by McAllo's remarks very much as if he had said that his grandfathers, by industry and thrift, had been able to hand him down a material property, and that finding it inconvenient to draw the interest, he was doing what he could to relieve himself by using his principal to back his luck at cards. There was a good deal of "bluff" in his allegations, and I need not have disturbed myself so much about them; but there was also an element of misapprehension which it seemed the Christian duty of any adult listener to correct. I don't know that he meant it so, but when he said "Puritanism," to my mind he meant the power of self-restraint and the ability to get along on the minimum of amusement. If McAllo has got these things in his blood, perhaps it is natural enough that, having never felt the lack of them, he should undervalue them, and wish to let a little of them out. But with you and me, who haven't got them by nature, perhaps, and have to secrete by personal, moral thrift all that we use, it is different. The tyranny of Puritan tendencies has no terrors for us. What worries us is the costly and unremitting obligation to keep ourselves amused, under penalty of dissatisfaction with life whenever we don't succeed. It seems as if a man with such forebears as McAllo's had nothing to do but to go out into the world with his sickle and reap. The hard work is beating one's recalcitrant self into a useful creature, responsive to one's higher aspirations and promptly obedient to the will.

For this poor, admirable McAllo, the chief part of that has been done. The lad likes by nature to learn, to work his brains, to live cleanly. He can have more fun with Homer and a student's lamp than a coarser-fibred lad can have with a bottle of champagne and a pool-table. Vulgar or vicious associates seem simply dull to him, and he can think more agreeable thoughts on milk and oatmeal than the average club man can on Pommery and terrapin. That is what a line of plain-living, high-thinking Scotchmen, now deceased, have done for him, and the poor ignorant boy knows no better than to grumble about his Puritan tendencies! If only they were marketable commodities, what a price he could get for them from some sad-hearted millionaire, who needs a new moral endowment for his son! If they were marketable he would learn quickly enough what they were worth.

In these days, when there is so much talk of heredity, we ought to recognize, as usually we do not, our obligations to the decent men and women from whom we have the good fortune to be derived. The ancestor who hands us down money gets recognition. He has done something that we can understand, and we name our children after him and try to keep his name before the world. But the saints in our family records—the men and women who have made a stand for us against sensuality and laziness—we do not half appreciate. It is a pity we are so dull. The wise king was as sagacious as usual when he said that a good name is rather to be chosen than great riches; but he was indisputably and obviously sagacious if, when he said "a good name" he meant good blood.

IX

CIVILIZATION AND CULTURE

CIVILIZATION AND CULTURE

Y friend Felix has been holding forth to me upon the importance of substituting, in thought and speech, the word "civilization" for the word "culture." "Culture," Felix says, is not so much what we need in this new country as "civilization." By civilization, as I understand him, he means something more than that we should eat with forks instead of knives. He means, I take it, that we should learn to be better worth talking to, better worth eating with, better worth living and associating with generally, and more worthy of being alive. Perhaps he feels as others have felt, that we lack distinction, and would have us get it, but whatever our need is, as he sees it, he doesn't think that "culture" expresses the

Felix clamors for "civilization" and disparages "culture."

means by which we may supply it. It is true that "culture" suggests somewhat exclusively the cultivation of the intellectuals, the reading of books, the study of languages, the hearing of hard music, and the inspection of difficult pictures. Felix does not deny that "culture," so understood, may help on the civilization that he cries out for, but he maintains that people may be civilized without being especially intellectual, and without attaining to any very notable flights of culture. To his sort of civilization, to know good books is a help, but hardly as much so as to know good people. Religion is a great power in promoting it. The arts and travel help it much; the sciences and trade not so directly. Yet people may be ever so learned, ever so pious, and travelled, and picture-wise, and yet not be civilized; so that to square with his ideal is no play-day undertaking.

And yet it is a useful ideal and worth taking some thought about. The people who are the most civilized may or may not be the worthiest people, but they are the pleasantest, and the ones who seem to get the most out of life. The French are undoubtedly better civilized than the Americans, and given the same apparatus, they are able to have more fun with it. In that particular they are ahead of the Americans; yet that they are worthier than the Americans is what even their hardiest admirer would hesitate to aver, and what no good American would admit for a moment. Their capacity for legitimate enjoyment seems to be greater than ours—for illegitimate enjoyment, too, it may be, but that we do not envy them. If they get more pleasure than we do out of talk, out of eating and drinking, out of art and music and the theatre, out of family life and their social relations generally, in respect to those matters their civilization is better than ours, and they are fit examples for our emulation.

While "culture," according to the common acceptance of it, is largely the cultivation of the mind, civilization, as Felix understands it, would seem to be the cultivation of the sympathies, the tastes, and the capacity for giving and receiving sound pleasures. The most civilized man is the man with the most catholic appreciation, the man who can be the most things to the most people, the man, to put it briefly, who knows best how to live. The man who is civilized can use all the culture he can get, but he can get on and still be civilized with a very moderate outfit of it. But the man who has culture and has not civilization is very badly handicapped. He may get a certain satisfaction out of living, but he will contribute only very moderately to the satisfaction of others. He may be respected, but he will hardly be cherished.

Provided he has books enough and is of an intellectual turn, a man may get culture all by himself, but he will hardly get a high degree of civilization except by rubbing against other persons. That is one reason why the most important of all civilizing agencies is the family. What libraries and picture-galleries are to culture, rightly regulated homes are to civilization. What a strong and thoroughly civilized family, that knows its business and improves its opportunity, can do toward the civilization of a raw American city, can only be appreciated after long residence in cities where such families do not exist. It should be an encouragement to Felix and a source of satisfaction to all of us that so sane an observer as Dr. Eliot, of Harvard, states as one of the chief bases of his hopes for the duration of our Republic, that "a better family life prevails among our people than was known to any of the republics that have perished, or, indeed, to any earlier century."

I believe that my cherished coeval Hoban Anson would find comfort in Felix and his theories about civilization. Hoban wants something very badly and his quest after it is earnest and continuous, but I don't think he knows exactly what it is, and if Felix could once explain to him that it was civilization I believe Hoban would believe him. I think he recognizes already that culture is not quite the thing he is after, but unless I mistake he is a little afraid still that it ought to be. He spends his summers far down in Maine, and has told me of the pleasure he finds there in the observation of the Yankee character, and in particular of the pursuit of culture under difficulties by some of the Yankee women. Hoban does not do his observing in any meagre fortnight, or even month, wrung from the exactions of business, but devotes whole summers to it—summers that begin late in the spring and merge liberally into autumn. The Maine village which he affects he describes as a place curiously, and, he thinks, providentially shielded from the contamination of the modern spirit by its geographical location. It had a vigorous marine life of its own before railroads were invented, and is so placed that, though a railroad might come to it, it could not advantageously pass through it. So the life has not run out of it, as it has out of many once prosperous New England villages, and it has kept much of its old Yankee stock in something like its old Yankee vigor. Hoban says for one thing that the Yankee voice, as he hears it there, has not the nasal tones that are com-

What Hoban Anson finds in Maine.

monly credited to it, but is clear and agreeable, but still Yankee in its inflections, and perhaps in its drawl. Besides that, he finds Yankee humor and Yankee independence very sturdy in quality, but qualified with a philosophical spirit and a patient, thrifty unwillingness to allow sentimental considerations to stand overmuch in the way of lawful gain. But what interests him as much as anything is the survival of the old Puritan conscientiousness, modified in its manifestations and transmogrified in its aims, but still persistent and effectual. As usual it is more obvious in the women than in the men, and it compels them rather to intellectual than spiritual flights. He complains that in their passion for self-improvement they set themselves awful tasks of reading, and labor through long, hard books with very much of the dreary persistence with which their forebears sat in cold meeting - houses under interminable discourses. Hoban is a product of Boston, and has come to middle life without any very protracted evasions of the atmosphere of his nativity. I have known him to read long books himself, but it seems to distress him that these Yankee women should devote to such tasks so much time and toil that, he thinks, might be more profitably employed. He told me that one of them said to him: "Oh, Mr. Anson, I do so envy you the opportunities for intellectual society that Boston must afford," whereat he had the grace to blush, remembering that almost the only overt indication of intellectuality that he gave at home was a constant and outspoken dissatisfaction with Boston newspapers, and a greedy preference for those of New York. He does not condemn this Yankee eagerness for culture nor deny that it bears some good fruit, but he seems to feel that in some degree it is a misdirected zeal, and that the fruits of it are not as filling at the price as they ought to be.

One civilizing agency which, I dare say, is operative in that Maine village where Hoban goes, but which is getting all too scarce in regions where culture is on top, is hymns. Your experience may be different, but the social circle in which I move is self-contained and unemotional to a degree that seems to preclude hymns, and I rarely hear them any more, except when I go to church. Then they are not sung, but "rendered" by surpliced specialists, into whose harmonies my ear may venture but not my voice. We are superior to a good many things in our set, and to hymns among others. Are hymns out of fashion, do you know, among the best people? When I was young we had them at home as regularly as bread and butter; but then we had family prayers too, and observed other ceremonies which now seem to be growing obsolete. I don't visit in any family where they sing hymns, except, to be sure, the family where I first heard them. I confess that I visit comparatively few families, and those comparatively worldly; but I often go out to supper on Sunday night with people who have been to church during the day, and I hear no hymns. The impression I gather is that there is more beer and champagne in the world than there was twenty-five years ago, and not so much devotional music; but one has always to be on his guard not to confuse personal changes with terrestrial movement, and especially not to mistake the signs of one's own individual degeneration for marks of the world's progress. I do not especially deprecate the beer, but I miss the hymns. They echo very pleasantly in the memory, and if the habit of singing them still holds in Maine that should be reckoned as one of the advantages of the aspiring Yankees who still lead simple lives there.

I think we are quite as pious in this generation as our forebears were, but our manifestations, though not less sincere than theirs, seem to be less overt. Most of us go to church, but we do not seem to attach the same importance to it as they did, nor to go quite so conscientiously. It is more of a habit with us and less of a duty, and if we find what seems a better occupation for a particular Sunday morning, our consciences do not smite us as sharply as consciences did thirty years ago. We are more apt than our fathers were to think that we know more about religion than the preacher does; and it may be that our impressions in that regard have foundation, for the latest news about matters of faith comes to us just as promptly as it does to him, and if it recommends itself to our belief there is less to retard our acceptance of it.

But if we are less sure than our parents were of getting our hymns in church, we ought to be less willing to forego them at home. It is painful to think of one's children growing up without hymns or hymn tunes in their heads, but that very thing may happen to them unless fit measures are taken betimes. The words of many modern popular hymns are absurd, and do violence to any reasonable person's intelligence; but the great hymns are sound poetry set to sound music, and though the sentiments of some of them do not altogether accord with the religious convictions of this enlightened generation, the greater number are as available now as they ever were, and the sanest singer need not mumble the words or make mental reservations as he sings them.

I believe that Felix, with his convictions of the need of civilization, and Hoban, with his misgivings about culture, would both agree with those informants who tell me that one of the most reassuring spectacles to be seen in New England last spring was my old friend and coeval, Robin Abner, out on his lawn of an afternoon, instructing and exercising his son Charles in the art of pitching a baseball. Fame and wealth crown the successful pitcher now, but there is no sordid taint about Robin's ambition for his son. His purpose is that Charles shall be a civilizing agency in the shape of an unsalaried pitcher on the Harvard nine, and I daresay that Charles will realize it. Robin, in his day, had aspirations of that sort for himself. I remember him twenty odd years ago on the ball-ground at Exover. The day I got my first sight of him, he was playing right field on the junior nine. He was long and strong and had yellow hair — practically yellow (he has none now—practically none)—and if his father had begun early and taken pains with him, as he is doing with Charles, I have no doubt that he would have made a great baseball player, and possibly a pitcher for

Robin Abner trains his son Charles.

the Harvard nine. As it was he was a fair player, but never eminent, for it was wartime when he was growing up, and his father, a great patriot and leader of men, was too busy prodding Massachusetts on to Richmond to give Robin's athletic education the attention it deserved. It made no vital difference, for Robin came out strong as it was.

You remember the story of how Chiron the Centaur had the raising of Jason, and of the pains he took to make him shoot straight with the bow and arrow. I dare say that the antediluvians who lounged in Chiron's back-yard on afternoons when he and Jason had their target up, were conscious of very much such sensations of reassurance as I get from the reports of Robin and Charles. When a serious-minded, burden-bearing man of business like Robin quits work to teach his son to pitch a ball, it makes me feel as if things were going to continue and progress, and as if the next generation might be good for something, and able to have some fun in spite of the growth of cities, and the spread of trolley-cars, and socialism and realism, and the new woman, and the concentration of wealth, and the multiplication of walking delegates, and all the varieties of devilment that solemnize the world's prospects. It makes it easier for me to hope that the learned gentleman named Nordau, who argues with so much plausibility about the demoralization and decadence of all of us folks, is needlessly alarmed.

If Robin were teaching Charles modern football, I should have my doubts about Robin's views of the future, and whether he thought it best that Charles should live to grow up. But baseball, a safe and stable and patriotic sport, is different, and the prospect that excellence in it is to become hereditary in the Abner family helps me to believe in the transmission of all sorts of sturdy virtues, and the development of many a good inheritance of strength. If the world wasn't a good world, and wasn't going to keep on being habitable, Robin would not care whether Charles learned baseball or not. Yet there he is with his coat off catching Charles's deliveries off of imaginary bats, and chiding him energetically when the ball goes wild.

I hope Robin will make a good thing, athletically, out of Charles. My son Nicodemus is growing up also, and though he is of a contemplative nature, and seems to prefer sitting down to more active exercises, I allow myself to hope that when Charles Abner stands in the pitcher's box on the Soldier's Field my Nicodemus will be there, and will be making a good report on the benches.

X

ARCADIA AND BELGRAVIA

ARCADIA AND BELGRAVIA

A CONTEMPORARY story-teller, who lays the scene of his narrative in Newport, reminds the reader that it was the Newport of departed days, "not the paradise of cottages and curricles, but of big hotels and balls, of Southern planters, of Jullien's orchestras and hotel hops." Newport had not become Belgravia then, but was something like Arcadia still.

I daresay that Belgravian Newport is amply satisfactory to its denizens as it is; but there is that in the coloring of the story which reminds one to lament not only the loss of the Arcadian Newport, but the general and inevitable tendency of all the more charming summer Arcadias to take on the Belgravian characteristics. Arcadia is ever unstable. It begins by being sylvan. The shepherds wear flan-

Belgravia's encroachment on Arcadia.

nel shirts, and the shepherdesses go about in big hats and tennis shoes, and wear the same dress all day long, and scarcely venture to tie a ribbon to their crooks. Quickly Arcadia gets the fame of being a pleasant place. People are so friendly there; manners are so easy and so good. Chaperons are scarce and high, and no one cares, for such Eden-like simplicity prevails that chaperons are not needed. Before long the people who have been overdosed with conventionalities and are tired of fine raiment hear of it. Word gets around that some of the nicest people go to Arcadia, and that there is no place where the girls have more fun, or where the youth are more eligible, or from which everybody brings home a finer color or better spirits in the fall. But what is money for if not to enable its owners to enjoy the newest delights? So soon as Arcadia's charms begin to be noised abroad the place begins to be the fashion. New-comers create new needs, and soon, far too soon, the shepherdesses are getting their gowns from Watteau and changing the ribbons on their crooks four times a day. The hotel quadruples in size, and is crammed full of Sybarites. Gradually the original Arcadians realize that society has grown too miscellaneous, and begin to put up separate huts and withdraw to them. Then the Sybarites discover that the hotel is primitive and countrified, and straightway build themselves cottages with rooms for many servants and stables for troops of quadrupeds. Then comes the short-tailed horse, and the British groom multiplies in the landscape. Champagne and chaperons surge in, hand in hand. Simplicity goes elsewhere and sells her abandoned tenement to Style, who pulls it down and puts up a palace on its site. And so Arcadia fades away and the sign "Belgravia" looms up in large letters at the railroad station.

And what becomes of all the true Arcadians who were happy once together? Some build fine houses on their property and rent them to Belgravians and go away themselves for the summer. Some put their sheep in charge of a hireling and supply the cottagers with spring lamb. Some hang up their crooks and go into the real-estate business, but many, perhaps most of them, are corrupted and turn Belgravians themselves. For Belgravian existence has an intoxicating quality about it that is able to upset the discretion of people who ought to know better. Even for the rich it is fairly debatable whether Belgravia is so happy a land as Arcadia, and for the poor there is no question at all about Arcadia's superiority. Yet it is constantly happening to the worthy poor whose choice has been Arcadia, to have the Belgravian current turn their way and sweep them off their legs. Belgravia is so insinuating. For what it lacks of being picturesque it makes up in being fine. Its standards are mere arbitrary conventions, and yet once one gives in at all to them they quickly come to have the force of natural laws. Inch by inch, substituting elegance for mere comfort and show for simple use, it lures the would-be Arcadian into a competition wherein it is a weariness to engage and an embarrassment to succeed. There are certain kinds of nuisances against which the promoters of

Arcadias take pains beforehand to provide, selling land only for uses and under conditions which they deem compatible with their general purposes. But they never provide against the chances of a Belgravian degeneration. They stipulate that no hut of less than a certain value shall be built upon the lots that they sell, but they never limit the prospective builder the other way. His edifice must come up to the prevailing standard, but nothing hinders him from so far surpassing it as to make all his neighbors feel that the conditions of their existence are squalid. Arcadias have been spoiled as Arcadias without ever reaching the full measure of Belgravian development. Promoters must know that, but they never guard against it. If the current sets Belgraviaward they take the chances of arrival, lamenting nothing, and seeming to feel, in business-like obtuseness, that simplicity has achieved its highest end if it has paved the way for fashion.

In the summer and autumn landscape of the passing hour one finds two comparatively new features, in the appreciation of which Belgravians and Arcadians have come closer together than has been their wont. Neither feature is brand new. One has been growing more and more familiar for a whole decade until now it is everywhere. That is the all-conquering bicycle, which goes persistently on its gainful course, holding its adherents, and daily gaining new victims.

Two new features of the landscape.

The bicycle's advance has been so gradual, so noiseless, and so easy that it is doubtful if American society appreciates what it is about or what are its possibilities. Starting as a toy, and continuing on a democratic basis as a means of transportation for the comparatively poor, it has worked its way steadily on and up. Sportsmen have scoffed at it; horsemen have flouted it; high dignitaries of the church have denounced it to their women adherents; solid citizens have held it to be a nuisance on the highway; timid people have deprecated its presence on the sidewalk, but it has rolled along practically unhindered, increasing in numbers, growing in popularity, until now it disputes with the horse for the patronage of fashion. It is time to take the bicycle seriously, as a thing, like the cotton-gin, the steam-engine, the telegraph, and the sewing-machine, that is to have an effect upon society.

As an annihilator of space it is the able coadjutor of the railroad. It deals with details, covering the distances which are too far to walk, and the ground which the steam-engine sweeps one past before he knows it. The ground one goes over on a bicycle he does know, hence it promises to bring back to human acquaintance the numberless nooks and corners of the civilized earth that the locomotive rushes by, and which have sunk out of ken since steam travel became universal. It is still a toy in some hands, but it is also a great vehicle, giving every performer (where the roads are good) an available door-yard at least ten miles square, and making fresh air and exercise more easily obtainable. At the same time it amuses the rider, and everybody knows how important it is that with one's air and exercise a share of amusement should be thrown in.

But the most startling tendency of the bicycle is its effect upon woman. As sure as taxes, or the destruction of the peach crop, or anything that is inevitable, it is about to emancipate that suffering creature from the dominion of skirts. No woman of sense will ever discard skirts altogether. They are far too seemly and becoming for that. But woman has marked the bicycle for her own, and no woman can ride on a bicycle without discovering that skirts have their place and their uses, and that there are times and situations where they are in the way. The habit of sea-bathing has done much to break down the tyranny of women's clothes. Bicycles will do the rest. Already the divided skirt is used by women on horseback without exciting the beholder's dismay, but that is not a fashion that gives assurance of extensive growth. But that the woman who rides bicycles will wear knickerbockers is a bit of concluded destiny; that once having found them acceptable for one form of exercise she may find them convenient for divers others is very possible, and yet not appalling, since

Arcadia and Belgravia

knickerbockers do not look ill. That she will dance in them, or dine in them, is not likely enough to give anyone valid grounds for anxiety, but once she has learned how, she will wear them without compunction on fit occasions where skirts too much restrain, as when she plays golf.

For the other new feature of the landscape is golf. Golf has been threatening to cross the seas these last five years. It came unobtrusively, and this year has fairly taken root and spread itself. All the country clubs have it. Veteran tennis-players have cast aside their bats and taken up with "drivers" and "putting-irons," and, more extraordinary still, horsemen of mature convictions are found tramping around golf-links day after day and spending the solid evening hours bragging of the strokes they made, and raising futile lamentations over scores spoiled by wanton misses. One does not fully realize the fascination of golf until he has heard it talked by confirmed horsemen in times when they might be talking horse. It commends itself as a serious sport, fit to engage the well-preserved but not too boisterous energies of the middle-aged, suitable for stout men to apply to the correction of obese tendencies, and yet not too violent for the spare frames of the thin. It is neither dangerous nor costly, and yet the philosophical mind finds satisfaction in it, while the sportsman admits that it possesses the indispensable qualities of a true game. There can be little doubt that it will possess all America as tennis has. It has the best literature of any known game, which is due possibly to its Scotch origin, and the instruments with which it is cultivated are of so fascinating an aspect that the palm instinctively itches to clutch them and see how they work. Once seen, golf cannot be forgotten; once experienced, it will not be neglected. It has fairly got us now, and it may be trusted to keep us.

The element of companionship enters seriously into golf. It enters considerably into most games, so that the majority of us care more whom we play with than what we play. But one could play tennis with any player whose skill approximated to his own without much thought of his personal idiosyncrasies, for the net yawns and stretches between tennis-players, keeping them apart; and while they are playing the action is too lively to permit the communication of anything but the ball. But a fit person to play tennis with is one thing and a thoroughly satisfactory person to play golf with is another. Ivan Putter, in whose society I had the good fortune to be thrown last summer, was such a person. This summer I did not have the advantage of his company, and at many holes I have grieved over our separation with wistful appreciation of his qualities as a golfer. It is true that he was no very great shakes with his clubs. I could drive farther than he could and put about as well, and though I did not win more than my share of games from him, I had always the solace of being persuaded that he was not really in my class at golf, and that any day when I was really myself and playing my game I could beat him. Somehow I was seldom myself and rarely played my game, whereas his game, such as it was, he was usually able to put up, so that the disparity between my estimate of his skill and my opinion of my own was not a real hindrance to our rivalry. But irrespective of his abilities with drivers and mashies he had traits of surprising value. For one thing he is an excessively lazy man, and always arranged beforehand for a good supply of caddies both for himself and me, and he trained his caddies — which were casual boys picked up haphazard — so well that they were an example to mine, and the standard of efficiency of the whole squad was high. Then he usually spent the evening in reading the golf rules and in making himself an authority on points of etiquette and play, with the result that my head was as little troubled with knowing the rules as it was with knowing the caddies. He took his game seriously, never trifling with a stroke, exulting when he made a good one, grieving when he didn't, and working hard all the time. And when he wasn't attending to his own game he was paying close attention to mine. That was perhaps his greatest charm. When it was my drive he waved out the fore caddies, advised me as to my tee, and stood over the stroke. If it was a good one it was doubly glorious. If it was a miss or a foozle he helped me swear. His interest kept mine always warm, so that I held almost as much of my breath over his strokes as he over mine. He insisted on perfect order in turns, and indeed on every propriety the rules suggested; and when there was a ball lost he abandoned it with the same reluctance when it was mine as when it was his.

A railroad crosses the links where Ivan Putter habitually plays. Mindful of his deliberation, I have dreaded all summer to hear that he had been run over by the cars between the cow-pasture and the home hole. But I hope he may be spared, for since I played with him I have played with other men, men who scurry helter-skelter across the fields, chasing their balls like terriers after tom-cats, men who know few rules and respect not those, men who pay little attention to their own play and none to mine, triflers, scorners of etiquette, ignorant and without a standard. They mean well enough, poor gentlemen, but how I wish they might be apprenticed for a time to Ivan Putter and learn to temper their methods with some of the graces of his admirable spirit.

When the Arcadian gets back to town.
Not the simplicity of Arcadia, nor the luxury of Belgravian Newport or Belgravian Lenox, not the attractiveness of new and sylvan bicycle paths, nor the superlative merits of a seashore golf links can avail for more than one or two short months to delude the summer vacationer from the city about the intensity of his own gregarious instincts. Any doubts he may have had about it are apt to be rudely dispelled, when, after his month by the sea or in the country, he first strikes a considerable town. It need not be such a very big town, but only a city with the ordinary appliances of city life, with hotels that are real hotels, not summer hotels; with shops, newspapers, and people. It is really pitiable to see the poor creature's satisfaction in finding the commonest appurtenances of urban existence within his

reach. The most ordinary sights bear a friendly aspect to him. The members of the Salvation Army that he sees in the streets seem to him like old acquaintances. The cigar-store Indians are his long-lost brothers. The conventional ornaments of the drug-stores, the soda-water fountains, and awful instruments, and sponges, and patent-medicine boxes that garnish those repositories, seem cheerful and alluring to him, and the familiar drug-store smell rises in his nostrils like the very breath of life. There are barber shops—he can have his locks trimmed; there are saloons—he can quench his thirst; there are bookstores—he can learn what progress literature has made during his absence from the world, and can look at the outsides of the newest books and supply himself with all the latest magazines. It rejoices him, as he dodges a trolley-car, to find his instinct of self-preservation still unimpaired. A bicycler grazes him as he whizzes by, and he swears more in glee than in irritation. Poor degenerate creature, after viewing God's creation for a month man's poor appliances possess a new charm for him. The visions he had in June of the delights of a lifelong communion with nature have faded out, and he rejoices that his lot has been cast in the haunts of men. Even his work, that he had come so to despise, has charms for him again, and he thinks with relief, and even with enthusiasm, of having a desk to return to every morning, and of the set task which is to occupy his active hours and relieve him of the obligation to choose between rival forms of laborious amusement.

Bless the man! Don't imagine that the merits and blisses and attractions which he sees in cities really exist. Don't suppose that the sight of the blue sea or the blue hills is not intrinsically better than any sights he will find in town. It is just a case of *cœlum non animum*, that's all. He is a bundle of habits like all of us, and it is because he is getting back to his habits that he rejoices. He is a machine, and however it may benefit him now and then to stop for a time and repair his several parts, he is happiest on the whole when he is running, and he runs easiest and most profitably in the place that he has learned to fit. He may pose for a few weeks every year as a human creature, but the truth is that he is a mere appliance, and best off, as his own instincts tell him, in the place where he can best be applied.

XI

OURSELVES AND OTHER PEOPLE

OURSELVES AND OTHER PEOPLE

 WRITER in a contemporary American magazine who compares English and American home life says that the most striking difference is that the chief end of an English home is the comfort of the man, but the chief end of an American home is the comfort of the woman. That accords with American tradition about the manners and customs of the English, and probably it is as nearly true as epigrammatical statements are wont to be. Still one may wonder whether it would not be almost as illuminating to suggest that the chief end of English homes is the comfort of the proprietors, while the ruling consideration in American homes is the propitiation of servants. Unless current information upon the subject is misleading,

English and American homes.

both master and mistress in an English home can buy much more domestic comfort than the same expenditure could gain for them in America; and that mainly for the trite reason that English servants are better trained, more easily procured, and cheaper than in America. The French Government lately proposed to raise an annual revenue of twenty-five million francs by a tax on domestic servants, to be paid by their employers. The tax is reported to be extremely unpopular among the servants, who say that they will have to pay it in the end; and the assertion that there are forty thousand of them out of employment in Paris indicates such a condition of the domestic labor market as seems to give a substantial basis to their fears. Americans would smile at the idea of being taxed for their servants. A bounty on each one would better suit the sentiments of the average American housekeeper. Not that life in the homes of well-to-do Americans is such a savage experience, or that servants are not indispensable in such homes, or that the house-keeper blames them for what neither she nor they can help at present, or that she undervalues their work; but merely because they are hard to get, hard to manage, and hard to keep, and expensive, and she wishes she did not have to have them. The Englishman's idea of domestic comfort may be an establishment with a dozen servants, but the average American woman's ideal is very few servants and good, and no more of an establishment than they are willing to take care of for her.

The English way of having comfort with servants is to have plenty of them, assign them definite tasks and not more than they can do well, feed them cheaply, and pay them low wages. The American way is to have fewer, feed them more expensively, pay them much higher wages, and expect a greater and less definite amount of service. The Englishman is satisfied with his method, provided he can gather income enough to carry it out. But the American is not satisfied, and a tolerably ample provision of funds does not cure his dissatisfaction. He does not think he gets his money's worth of comfort, and it is quite possible that he is right.

There will be a cure presently for this predicament, but it will not come on any considerable scale through a closer approximation of his domestic methods to those of the English. It will have to be a cure that will be quite as popular with the servants as with the masters. The grandchildren of this generation will get more domestic comfort for less money than their grandparents did, and one reason why will be that they will have a much more accurate notion of what they want and what they are entitled to. Standards of living will be much more definite in America two generations hence. Servants' rights, duties, privileges, and wages will all be better defined. House-keepers will know much more exactly and without need of personal experience what scale of living their incomes can support. Rents will be lower, and there will be a better notion than now as to what household luxuries and conveniences are really luxuries and conveniences, and what are mere showy impediments to domestic comfort. With a great and growing body of intelligent people anxious to work, and an increasing number anxious to have certain work done for them, the adjustment of the supply of labor to the demand is bound to be perfected. And yet it will be an American adjustment, with somewhat less servility in it than in the English method, and characterized, as all other American labor is, by the superior efficiency of the persons employed.

Among other vexed questions relating to personal service which we may hope to see settled in that glad coming time when everybody will know more than anyone knows now is the matter of "tips." It needs settling, for it is a good deal discussed and opinion is divided upon it. Not long ago a contemporary scribe in discussing the employment of college students as waiters in summer hotels complained of " the avidity with which they accept money from people who are their intellectual and social inferiors." It was this writer's conviction that " no person of refined sensibilities will accept a 'tip.'" Now, to be over-eager for fees is not consistent either with self-respect or with good service, but there seem to be good reasons to differ from the opinion that to accept gratuities offered in recognition of personal services is necessarily inconsistent with a serviceable degree of refinement.

The ethics of "tips." As between a self-respecting guest and a self-respecting servant, a fee is not a bribe, but an expression of appreciation. It is a tangible way of saying Thank you! When a gentleman has been a guest in another gentleman's house, and his comfort has been a special charge of certain of his host's servants, the fees he may choose to give those servants when he goes away simply say that he appreciates their care of him, and is grateful. Such fees are not alms, nor are they bribes; they discharge an obligation which, whether it actually exists or not, is recognized as equitable by the departing guest. Fees of that sort, freely and cordially given, and expressive of good-will, are a source of satisfaction to the giver, and it is not apparent why they should not be a perfectly legitimate source of satisfaction to the receiver also.

It is true that when the departing guest comes to say good-by to his host he does not tip him. He thanks him for his hospitality, and very likely expresses the hope that he may soon be able to return it in kind. He has toward his host a feeling of obligation analogous to what he has toward his host's servants. He knows that first or last he will get even with his host by showing him some courtesy or doing him some service, but the chances are that unless he discharges the obligation he feels to the servant by a material gift on the spot no other opportunity to requite him will offer.

The "tip" given to a servant by an appreciative guest is given to the office rather than to the individual. It is not charity, and to accept it need not necessarily offend the self-respect of the most self-reliant person. There is no lack of other vocations besides "service" in which fees, more or less gratuitous, are given without the slightest loss of self-respect on either side. The clergyman who marries a couple gets a fee, and is entitled to it, but whether it is five dollars or five hundred depends entirely on the feelings and pecuniary abilities of the groom. To perform the marriage ceremony, even when it includes the salutation of the bride, isn't very hard work, and it would be reasonable to say that anything over twenty-five dollars, or perhaps less, that the clergyman gets is in the nature of a gratuity. But whether his fee is fifty dollars or a hundred, he never feels obliged to send any part of it back. It is given to his office rather than to himself, and his office enables him to accept it without remorse or impropriety. To stickle for a large fee would be decidedly improper. A well-behaved clergyman does not permit his mind to dwell unduly on his marriage fees one way or the other, and he is ready to marry folks as securely and reverently without money or price as he would for the most lavish remuneration. But what fees come to him unsolicited he puts into his pocket cheerfully and without a qualm, conscious that the laborer is worthy not only of his hire, but of any casual pecuniary barnacles that happen to stick to it.

And so with the office of servant. It is called a humble office, but it is as capable as any other of being adorned in the manner of its discharge. The best servant is the one who is most successful in promoting the comfort of the people he serves. If he appreciates the possibilities of his office and lives up to them, there is no reason why the casual emoluments of it should burn his fingers. If he spends himself generously in his work, he has no more valid reason to feel humiliated by the offer of a fee than the clergyman is when the best man hands him an envelope. If his sensibilities are too refined to permit him to accept fees, that is not a merit, but a defect, and he is that much less fit for the place that he holds. A servant who demands fees or whose usefulness is measured by the acuteness of his expectations is a nuisance and an imposition, but a servant to whom a considerate guest cannot express a sense of gratitude has a defective conception of his job.

If a man or a woman doesn't want to serve for money, and can find means of avoiding it, by all means let them. But if any one, even a person of the most refined sensibilities, undertakes to be a servant, it is better for such a one to try to be the best servant possible, accepting the casual emoluments of the office with the same goodwill with which he undertakes his duties.

Japanese manners. No doubt the Japanese, whose example in so many particulars is nowadays so freely held up for our emulation, have considered the question of tipping and come to some conclusion about it which it might be advantageous for us to know. We hear very much of the Japanese, and most of what we hear is greatly to their credit. They have many nice qualities and a fair share of great ones. They are clean, they are polite, and apparently they are very gentle and very brave. They are said to be exceedingly neat, too, and to be bountifully endowed with that sense of propriety, a defective development of which accounts for much of the rubbish on American streets and most of the disagreeableness of American street-car travel. They certainly beat us in a good many things. Intelligent foreigners who have observed us closely have declared that we are the rudest and the kindest people in the world. Of course it is a pity that we are not more universally courteous; that our children are not demure and orderly like the Japanese children; that we throw papers into the street and drop peanut-shells and orange-peel on the floors of our public conveyances. Of course it is a pity that we are not more like the Japanese in many particulars; but, for my part, I make bold to confess that American manners, with all their defects, are better suited to my American taste than Japanese manners with all their gentle perfections.

When Nature finds bark necessary for the protection of her growths it may be noticed that she always applies it to the outside. Our manners are to a certain extent our bark, and though it is by no means necessary that it should be disagreeably rough or scraggy, it seems not a thing to be altogether deplored that what we have of it we should choose to wear as the trees do, externally and in sight. When Nature leaves the bark thin she is apt to provide thorns, and if one must make a choice between the two means of protection, it may be excusable to prefer the bark which one can recognize afar off, to the thorn which draws blood without warning.

We are quite accustomed to the traditional disparagement of the French as a people in whom a superficial politeness is developed at some cost of more indispensable merits, but the politeness of the Japanese being a trait of comparatively recent observation, seems to be accepted without much consideration of its cost. It is worth much, but it does cost something. For one thing, travellers tell us that it takes a prodigious amount of time. Japanese etiquette takes no note of the hands of the clock, or the rising or the setting of the sun. Japanese business seems not to be very much prompter. Time in Japan is estimated at its Eastern value. We are told, too, that Japanese courtesy condemns even such a reasonable candor as would permit one in polite conversation to acknowledge that he held an opinion different from one his friend had expressed, and that letters are not punctuated in Japan because it would seem to imply ignorance in the recipient. There can scarcely be such an extreme softness of conduct without some sacrifice of downright honesty.

American manners are not nearly as good as they should be, not nearly as good as one may hope they may become, but that Japanning would profit them is not so certain as it looks at first sight, even if it did not involve a much greater amount of self-repression or self-obliteration (doubtless more apparent than actual) than the American temperament could endure or has any desire to attain to. The amelioration of our national demeanor must rather be sought in an increased and enlightened self-control joined to a strengthened self-respect. If we ever do become civilized, it will be first at the heart and afterward at the rind.

Cousin Anthony and I

Reputed French traits.

If we had been imitative enough to learn manners by observation, we might have profited more by what we have seen of the French, but an obstacle to that has long existed in the shape of a vulgar sentiment about the French people, held mainly by Englishmen and Americans under the shadow of English thought, which was tersely though somewhat crudely expressed by the man who became dissatisfied with the conduct of a French waiter in a restaurant and noted the ever-recurring solace he found in the belief that all Frenchmen when they died would go to hell. The author of "French Traits" has been at pains to make it clear that this conception of the destination of the French is probably erroneous, and is based on ignorance of French character. He boldly maintains that the French are not wicked in all the particulars in which they differ from the English, but in some are merely different. Especially, he points out, the Frenchman has the social instinct in a degree that the Anglo-Saxon can neither aspire to nor easily comprehend, and many details of conduct which we attribute to the defects in his character are really due to the exceptional development of his solidarity. Thus, if he is somewhat querulous and unduly prone to vociferation, that is not because he is really more quarrelsome than his Anglo-Saxon neighbor, but that, thanks to his dependence on his fellow, his wrath evaporates in language, whereas British individualism comes to blows. And if his moral sense, and even his moral conduct, digresses from the British ideal, that is due, if not directly to his solidarity, at least to the same causes that have made him the social creature that he is.

It is a great comfort to a humane mind of Anglo-Saxon perversions, to find out these peculiarities of the French, and learn to regard their future, whether in this world or the next, with hopefuller anticipations. So much relief comes to a benevolent intelligence from a comprehension of the reasons that exist for believing that a great contemporary people are not so wholly abandoned as they seem, that it naturally occurs to try the same prescription for the cure of what seem to be analogous cases. And in particular there are the Irish. Some of us Americans and many of our British cousins are worried about the Irish. We Americans especially are liable to forebodings that they are too quarrelsome, or too improvident, or too imperfectly veracious, or too something else to make up into American citizens of the proper standard. How immensely reassuring it would be to all of us who want to hold the best opinion that is tenable of our fellow-countrymen, if some one, taking a leaf out of " French Traits," would take the pains to demonstrate that the Irish have got solidarity, too, and that there is nothing really the matter with them, but only something different. To say that the French are all going to the bow-wows, and the Irish are in some respects very like them, is one thing. But to say that the French have the eminently precious and respectable quality called solidarity in a condition of exalted development, and the Irish have it also, is quite a different sentiment. As fast as we learn to feel like that about it we are filled with an increasing eagerness to take the Celt to our bosoms, and enjoy the benefits of solidarity at his expense.

If the Irishman had not some qualities that were exceptionally worth investigation, we Americans would not have him so much on our minds. His political importance in this country would not be so disproportionate to his numbers and his wealth, unless there were some points in which he had the advantage of the rest of the population. Is it not really his solidarity, nursed and developed by the same Catholic Church that has helped the same development in France, that enables him to carry the ward, and prove himself

> The very pulse of the machine,

while his Yankee brother, wrapt in his individualism, looks on somewhat jealously, and wonders how it is done!

XII

PROFIT AND LOSS

PROFIT AND LOSS

OUR vigilant newspapers keep close track of the great sales of pictures and bric-à-brac which occur from time to time in Europe, and give daily reports of the more important articles bought, and the prices paid for them. It might seem as if such reports were of interest only to collectors, and very rich collectors at that, for the total sum realized at such sales often runs up into the millions, and the average price of single pieces often approaches a thousand dollars. Nevertheless, it is edifying for a philosopher of moderate income to follow them, because of the important testimony they give of the vast number of expensive things that people who cannot afford to buy them can get along just as comfortably without. The assurance that millions of dollars can easily

Things one can do without.

be spent for things, no one of which is indispensable, or even highly important, to human happiness, is always fit to make the citizen whose circumstances are merely moderate less restless in the circumscribed limits of his earthly lot. To have all the Spitzer treasures sold, and not to have bought even one of them, and still to find life remunerative and satisfactory, is a gainful experience, and one worth some newspaper reading to acquire.

An experience of the same sort was possible at the Chicago fair. There one saw thousands of beautiful and costly objects fit to delight the eye and stimulate the imagination. To see all and to buy nothing, and still to come home justified and content, richer for what one's mind could carry away and very little poorer in one's pocket, was a possibility which was within every fair-goer's reach, and which the great majority realized. And it was worth realizing, if only for its use in helping them to recognize the agreeable truth that the material things that are essential to satisfactory existence are comparatively few and comparatively cheap. The capacity to recognize that, vividly and practically, is an acquirement fairly comparable in value with accumulations in the bank.

Moreover, it is a feasible acquirement. It can be taught. There is no certain possibility of making a phenomenal money-getter out of even an exceptionally intelligent boy, but it is fairly within the province of education so to train a lad that he can get more pleasure and far more profit out of a little money than another of inferior training can out of much. To be "passing rich on fifty pounds a year" is an accomplishment not readily attainable in the present state of money values; but to be richer on five thousand dollars a year than another man is on fifty thousand may not be as easy as lying, but it is easy enough. The necessaries of life are food, shelter, and raiment; the more important luxuries are cleanliness, books, society, good clothes, and a reasonable amount of leisure. In order to live his best, man wants time to think and plenty to think about. A moderate amount of travel is a luxury that enlivens the intellectual processes and is favorable to health. All the necessaries are easily procurable in these days, and none of the reasonable luxuries are very dear. The things that cost much money are chiefly those that delight the eye, and gratify not so much by use as by mere possession. One does not have to own rich things to enjoy them. The very best of them are in public collections, and abundance of others, in private hands, are not hard to get a sight of. It is more or less the same with that other grade of superfluities to which belong horses and yachts, truffles, pâté de foie gras, terrapin, canvasback ducks, champagne, English grooms, valets, and everything that contributes to make idleness palatable. There is undoubtedly some fun to be had with these objects, which do possess a certain sort of intrinsic value; but it is true of some of them, as it is of vases and pictures, that you can get the usufruct of them without owning them, since if a man drives two grooms and four horses it costs you nothing to see him go by. For the rest it may be said that there is just as much enjoyment of a different sort to be had without these things, and whether the cheaper or the more expensive pleasures are really preferable is simply a matter of education and taste. Consideration of the ease with which the five-thousand-a-year man can go without every one of the luxuries for which his neighbor, who has fifty thousand a year, spends four-fifths of his income, is fit to give the reflecting observer some useful ideas. The life of a family on two hundred dollars a year is immensely superior to existence on one hundred. Life on five hundred is a vast improvement on life on two hundred. Life on a thousand a year is much easier and more satisfactory than life on five hundred. Life on five thousand is still simple enough, and offers more opportunities and better ones than life on one thousand, and brings more leisure and seems more desirable on many grounds. But then the consumption of superfluous luxuries has already begun, and possibly the point has already been passed that was coveted by the ancient who desired neither

<small>*The cost of living.*</small> poverty nor riches. It would be a duller world if no one could spend more than five thousand a year, and far be such a condition from obtaining. Still, having even no more than that, there is no general certainty that increased expenditures will buy the money's worth; that they will make life more wholesome or more satisfying to the expenders; that they will promote health or the development of character, or cause love and peace any more to abound. Enough may not be as good as a feast. Indeed, it isn't. But, even if it consists merely of oatmeal and boiled eggs, it may easily be immensely better than a steady diet of feasting. Somewhere between a hundred dollars a year and unlimited means, money ceases to be a means of buying what is good for you and becomes an opportunity, which grows more and more difficult to improve as its size increases, until, if worse comes to worst, it may assume the proportions of an impossible task.

But, of course, there are always multitudes of us who are not only willing to undertake that task, but are constantly on the lookout for chances, the shrewd improvement of which may possibly advance us toward a position where we may test its hazards and drawbacks. Few people hope to get rich by the slow process of earning and saving, but there are multitudes of us whose imaginations are equal to the feat of forecasting the amplification of our resources by judicious investment. There is a great deal that is queer about investors. They have peculiar characteristics, or, perhaps, it would be nearer right to say that the occupation they follow has peculiar characteristics which they illustrate. There have been many good men since Colonel Newcome's time who have been bad investors, and many bad men who have been good investors. I suppose there have also been, and are, many good men who are good investors, and whose investments have not involved them in conduct at variance with the rules of ethics that ordinarily govern good conduct. Very astute men they must be, or very lucky, or both.

A person who had been invited to invest

a sum of money in a project which promised gratifying returns, was disposed to do so, but bethought him to advise first with an investor of large experience. The investor's advice was adverse, partly because he learned that his inquirer had no money in hand and convenient to lose, and partly because the project did not altogether please him. One of his objections that impressed the inquirer was this. He said: "It is not listed stock, and not easily marketable. If it starts to go wrong, you can't get rid of it. Now, if it were something that you could dump on the market when it began to weaken, you could get back part of your money at least."

Investors and their morals. Now, the adviser was a man in whose integrity the inquirer had very great confidence, for he knew him to be a churchwarden, as well as president of a bank. He noted, therefore, as a fit thing to be remarked, that a man of whom more than ordinary scrupulousness was to be expected, took it as a matter of course that an investor whose investment seemed likely to prove disastrous should get out from under it with the least possible delay, and try to let the loss fall on someone else. He didn't mind this sentiment in the bank president, but in the church-warden it seemed a misfit, as being contrary to the Golden Rule. Yet he was perfectly aware that it was a sentiment of all but universal prevalence, and that it was exceedingly unbusinesslike to cavil at it. So he went his way and eventually took two-thirds of his friend's advice, in that he only invested in the project that he was considering a third of what he originally hoped to put in. It happened just as the bank president said, that when the bottom fell out of the project (which happened cruelly soon) there was no getting rid of that stock at any price. But, so far as that went, the investor averred to himself that he was glad of it, and he really got a good deal of solace out of the feeling that, whatever was the size of his financial misconception, at least he was going to pay the whole cost of it himself.

It is a very common thing for people to lament that they did not get rid of this or that property before its value depreciated.

Of course, what they are really sorry for is that they could not have contrived to saddle their loss on someone else. It is a sign of the imperfection of contemporary benevolence that good people should have such feelings and should regard them as matters of course. They are humorously unchristian. The utmost the average investor-moralist enjoins is that a man shall not "unload" upon his friends. He cannot so much as imagine a scruple about selling out cadescent stocks in open market.

It will not be so when the millennium comes. Property will continue then, as now, to fluctuate in value, but the prospect of a depression will no longer strike the owner as a good reason for selling out. His superior moral sense will then, as now, be sometimes profitable to his estate, since property doesn't always depreciate as much as is expected, and often in the end it recovers more than it lost. But the great advantage from a business point of view of the perfected altruism will be the emancipation of the altruist from panic and all its consequences, since the man who is more ready to accept his loss than to pass it on is not to be scared into a foolish sacrifice by the shadow of it beforehand.

What the investor would choose is to put his money into some enterprise which shall cause two blades of grass to grow where one grew before, or several gold dollars to come out of the ground in place of one that goes in. Tradition and experience agree that a man who does that is a benefactor of his fellows and is entitled to enjoy both the profits of his enterprise and the pleasant emotions which are automatically incident to benevolent acts. But the average investor is not unduly exacting, and if he can have his profits, he is usually able to worry along without the consciousness of benevolence. If he cannot have his wish and make two blades of grass grow in place of one, he will be apt to consider, if he happens to possess broad meadows, that the next best scheme for him to promote is a contrivance through which it may come about that three blades of grass shall be needed to do the work of two. There is a vast field for investment in the work of supplying necessities that already exist, but another very pretty line of business is that which concerns itself with the invention of new necessities and the gratification of their demands.

It was in this latter sphere of endeavor that that clever and successful artist, the late Charles Frederick Worth, made a great reputation and a fortune for himself, and contributed more or less directly to the provision of profitable investments for very many others. Worth was pre-eminent among all his contemporaries as a designer of fashions in women's clothes. In so far as he devised beautiful gowns which adorned and beautified the women who wore them he did well. But the beautification of women is only a small part of the business of the inventor of fashions. What he relies upon for his pecuniary success is the artful cultivation of the human, and especially the feminine, passion for change. If women were allowed to wear their clothes as long as they were wearable, as men and snakes do, thrift would have a much better chance to develop and do its work,

The expensiveness of fashion.

than is consistent with the pecuniary interests of trade. The condition of servitude to which the arbiters of fashion have reduced womankind throughout nearly all of Christendom is a thing that it mortifies the spirit to remark. My Cousin Anthony was speaking of it not long ago. He said he was riding in a street-car one cold night in March with Mrs. Anthony, when he observed that her outside garment seemed inadequately warm. " For the first time it occurred to me," he said, " that I did not remember to have seen my wife in a fur coat since the winter began. But I knew that she had such coats in some variety, so I questioned her about it. Do you believe that she told me that none of her fur coats had either sleeve-room enough to admit the sleeves of her present dresses, or skirts of sufficient length to meet the requirements of the reigning mode? So she had been compelled to put away all of her furs in camphor, to lie until the fashions should come around, and meanwhile she went clad in such an inexpensive and insufficient top-garment as hard times permitted her to provide."

Mrs. Anthony is a very sensible woman who would not discard a warm and handsome jacket because of any mere whim. The force that constrains her to leave her furs in the attic and go out on a cold day in a cloth coat must be a force of compelling quality, and effectual to regulate the behavior of a lamentably large percentage of the Christian women of the time.

If only fashion had died with Worth we might mourn for him with a better-spared-a-better-man resignation; but his accomplices have survived him. Fashion will tyrannize over sorrowing households as absolutely as ever; shivering matrons will continue to leave their last year's fur coats at home, the march of the modes will go triumphantly forward, and shrewd inventors will continue to profit by it even though penury and disease may straggle in its wake.

XIII

CERTAIN ASSETS OF AGE

CERTAIN ASSETS OF AGE

A RECENT writer, discoursing "On Growing Old," took what seems to be a needlessly disparaging view of that inevitable process. He quoted Cicero's deliverances on the subject, but quoted them chiefly to scoff at what he affected to regard as the Roman essayist's faint praise of an indefensible condition. Cicero was thankful to old age because it diminished his appetite for food and drink, and aggravated his eagerness for rational conversation ; but this contemporary pessimist declared his belief that there was not an old man of his acquaintance who would not prefer roast fowl and champagne with the appetite and digestion of youth to the chance of conversing at length with the wisest person in the vicinity. Cicero con-

Some advantages of growing old.

sidered emancipation from physical appetites and passions as the best gift of old age, and this critic admitted that advantage, and added to it the felicity of escaping from "a certain tyranny of the intellect" and the privilege of having "no final convictions." But with all its compensations conceded, the decline of life seemed to him a poor thing, and fit chiefly to bring one to a penitential realization that life is a disappointment and vanity, and the mortal coil an integument chiefly blessed in the shuffling.

Now it was an amusing circumstance that this discourse should have come out in print sandwiched between some Reminiscences of Emerson, by Dr. Furness, of Philadelphia, and certain recollections of his college days by Dr. Edward Everett Hale. It appeared, from reference to Dr. Furness's article, that his experience of life covered at that time no fewer years than ninety-one. Dr. Hale's admissions made him out only a little over seventy, which is not old age, to be sure, but constitutes a reasonable maturity. Yet it was impossible to detect in the papers of either of these reverend and experienced gentlemen — one venerable and the other mature — any hint or suggestion that, so far as either of them had gone, he found any serious defect in life. This is not conclusive evidence, of course, but it is suggestive. It is particularly suggestive of one asset of old age which the essayist I have been talking about has omitted to specify. Everyone knows what the tontine system of life insurance is. A number of people pay equal sums of money into a pool ; the amount is put out at interest and the surviving subscriber takes the accumulated sum. Similarly, every man of letters gradually comes to be joint owner with other persons of a mass of valuable literary material which cannot be used by any of the joint owners so long as the others survive. But if he outlives the rest it all becomes his, and he can do what he will with it, without fear of hurting anyone's feelings or disclosing anything that would work injury to the living or to the memory of the dead. Who is there that writes and is still under fifty who will not admit that the stories he knows the best, and that are the best worth telling, are those that he cannot tell, because of the score of people still on earth who would strip the disguises from his characters and read as biography what he designed to have pass as fiction? Which of us does not think he might do a *magnum opus* if there were no lives in being to hinder!

And another great advantage of getting decently old is the acquisition of the privilege of loafing without compunctions. In these days, provided a man has fairly filled his granary during the heat and labor of his day of strength, old age is the time for him to travel, to own a farm, to collect books and china-images, to read many novels and frivolous books, to have a yacht if his accumulations will stand it, and to work just so much as will increase his contentment, and no more. He ought to have income enough to play with, and life enough left to play. If he hasn't, it is not the fault of old age, but of himself; or possibly it is his misfortune. Certainly old men abound who, having lived wisely and well, lack neither the means nor the disposition to find continued felicity in life. Anyone can recall a dozen such veterans at thought, and it would be easy to mention one or two whom everyone knows about, who in the ripeness of their intellectual and the haleness of their physical powers, seem to have more fun in a few minutes than many dull youths with good appetites have in a year.

The last years of Dr. Holmes seemed so notable for their felicities as to make them a shining instance of what the closing period of life ought to be.

Dr. Holmes was not one of those men of whom one feels that they should have lived to read their own obituaries, so as to have the satisfaction of knowing how greatly they were esteemed. He has been so widely and cordially appreciated for so many decades, that all the columns of matter the newspapers printed about him could scarcely have told him anything he did not know before. Whether poets find a personal pleasure in the appreciation of remote posterity is somewhat uncertain ; but there is no doubt that

Dr. Holmes and Boston.

the clamor of palm smiting palm is one of the most agreeable sounds that can fall upon a poet's living ear. Dr. Holmes was one of the most intelligently applauded poets that ever lived. If his poems of occasion are unmatched in felicity, it is largely because they had the great good fortune to be addressed in almost every instance to audiences of most exceptional ability to detect a hit. Boston has lost the dearest and most loyal of her old friends. Give her credit for what she did for him. She was loyal as well as he. What he had the wit to write and to say she had the discernment to appreciate. If Boston had not been Boston, Holmes could not have been Holmes. A Milton blind and solitary could write " Paradise Lost " and find the rapture of his own imagination a sufficient incentive. An Edwards in a rural village scarcely emerged from the primeval woods could meditate upon the nature and purposes of the Creator, and find the nature of his theme sustain his efforts. But a poet who writes to please must have an audience that is worth pleasing. Dr. Holmes was a poet of that sort, and it was one of his greatest felicities that from early youth he never had to seek for fit and friendly hearers. His thoughts never went unuttered for want of ears that invited their disclosure. He never had a good thought but that there was a good man within reach to share it with.

It is a matter of accepted tradition that poets are born, not made ; but not all the born poets are developed. Holmes beyond question was a born poet, but Boston may fairly be said to have raised him. He grew up under her wing. He was educated at her door. His first fame was won by verses first published in a Boston newspaper. He left her for a little while in early manhood, but she hastened to call him back, and provided him with a congenial task that suited his own needs as well as hers and kept him by her ever afterward. It is not surprising that he loved her or that she loved him. They were admirably mated. She made him happy and he made her famous, and incidentally made himself famous at the same time. Her occasions were his opportunities, and he met them with a continuing flow of felicitous response such as no poet of modern times has rivalled. Wherever Holmes is known Boston is known too. Her debt to him is fit to be compared to Scotland's debt to Walter Scott. If the long walk in her Common and the gilded dome of her State House are landmarks in literature it is because he made them so. No other American city ever had such a laureate; even Boston herself is not likely to have such another. The material for laureates is scarce nowadays; the inspirations are scarcer still, and Boston is not a family of New Englanders any more. She has outgrown that phase of her existence and is a great American city, too big and rich and overgrown and spread out, and with too miscellaneous a population to inspire again the sort of affection that old Boston stirred in Dr. Holmes. But she is entitled to the comfort of remembering that she recognized the laureate she did have, and that if his constancy never wavered, neither did her appreciation ever wane.

XIV

THE AFTER-DINNER SPEECH

THE AFTER-DINNER SPEECH

 CONTEMPORARY who discourses from day to day with zest, and often with wisdom, on all topics under the sun, said something the other day about the after-dinner speech. He pointed out how it must not be wholly facetious, nor frivolous, nor silly, nor too long-winded, nor highly exciting, nor over-heavy, nor ultra-argumentative, nor entirely statistical, nor in the least rancorous, but that it may contain some essential thoughts, some strokes of humor, some scraps of knowledge, some bits of fancy, some sound reasons, some good whims, some green dressing, and a little fat. He guessed that as many as five thousand after-dinner speeches had been made in New York during the season then closed, and recorded that one

The after-dinner speech.

man had made ten in a single week and three in one evening. He said he had heard a few tip-top after-dinner speeches, but they must have been a few out of many, for he spoke of hearing a considerable variety of others that for stated reasons were not tip-top. He remarked that a good many men had won renown by making clever after-dinner speeches, and mentioned four distinguished New Yorkers among whom the palm for after-dinner discourse was thought to lie.

There is no doubt that the after-dinner speech has grown to be an institution of serious magnitude. Its requisites are recognized to be such as the contemporary quoted has set forth. There are certain particular things that ought to go into it, and a lot of others that ought to be kept out. To combine the requisite ingredients so as to produce the proper flavor, and to serve the whole with felicity and grace, is a matter of such profound dexterity, and so few people ever attain it, that there seem to be reasonable grounds for the belief that the after-dinner speech, unqualified by a

The After-Dinner Speech

special purpose, is, for sober-minded and responsible citizens, little better than a trap. Indeed, there be those who hold that as an institution it is a fetish to which our sacrifices are altogether out of proportion to the returns. For a dinner with a special purpose some premeditated after-dinner talk is doubtless excusable. If we dine in the interests of politics, it is a legitimate part of the plan that some one should talk politics to us, and that we should sit under it. If we dine for charity, some one has a right to talk charity; and so analogously if we dine in the interests of education or trade. But if we merely dine for fun, why should we sit under any one? It would seem to be a needless disparagement of the inward working of any company of gentlemen, that after they had eaten their food it should be necessary to have persons especially deputized to think their thoughts for them. Why do they eat? Why do they drink? Is it merely to fatten them? Is it not that pleasant emotions shall be stirred inside of them, and that their individual tongues shall wag and their souls flow? But whose tongue can wag while Jones or Robinson is standing on his legs making oratory for the company, or whose soul can flow while Smith's psychological expansion is taking up all the space?

It is admitted that when there is really something to be said after dinner it is excusable to say it, but there is no lack of evidence that stated oratory, merely and exclusively for the promotion of digestion, is perilous alike to the gentlemen who undertake it, and to the object which it is intended to effect. For, as to the speakers, not every ordinary after-dinner talker understands that his function is to say nothing, but merely to talk. Some say something because they know no better; some because they have not the gift of utterance without communication; some from malice prepense because the devil prompts them; and some because they are carried away by the allurements of the opportunity. There is a story about a man in Philadelphia, a physician, who got up at a friendly dinner to talk digestively about nothing at all, when unexpectedly, not being enough on

The After-Dinner Speech

his guard, he let slip an idea. Once it was loose, he could not break away from it. It took possession of him. In a minute or two he was standing on his chair. In a couple of minutes more he was standing on the table, with all the after-dinner sleepers wakened up, and all the company silenced and fixed upon him with their eyes. He made a great speech, the memory of which still survives, but as an after-dinner speech it was a failure, for it stopped digestion short in over forty Philadelphia stomachs, and a dozen worthy gentlemen went to bed that night with dyspepsia.

And besides the risk of saying something, there is always the hazard of saying the wrong kind of nothing. That is a peril to which serious-minded men are particularly exposed, and is the one to which, a year or two ago, Justice Brewer and Justice Brown, of the United States Supreme Court, fell victims. Justice Brewer, it seems, went to a Yale dinner somewhere during the Christmas holidays, and appreciating, perhaps, the propriety of suiting his discourse to his auditors, he said things, the condemnation of which greatly abounded in the newspapers for some time afterward. So with Justice Brown, who was charged with sacrificing to his after-dinner necessities the sacred dignity of the very bench on which he sat, and with making allusions to his brother judges fraught with reprehensible gayety. It was not really the fault of these worthy and learned men that they got into such a scrape. The blame belonged to an undiscriminating institution which exacts intellectual skirt-dancing from elephantine intelligences.

Of the personal distress which after-dinner oratory brings on the unaccustomed after-dinner orator, it is hardly necessary to speak. Most of us know too much about that from personal experience. Between the necessity of saying something and the obligation to say nothing in particular; between the need of drinking enough to be fluent and the importance of not drinking enough to be incoherent; between the obligation to be entertaining and the hazard of being indigestible, it is not surprising that broken rest and an uneaten dinner

The After-Dinner Speech

should be the raw orator's lot. When he has become thoroughly hardened he doesn't mind. But think of the cost of hardening him! It is another case of the hatful of spoiled eyes which bought the oculist his experience.

For all the sorrowful hours which the contemporary American has spent or may live to spend sitting under after-dinner orators who know not what to say nor when to stop, he has himself to blame. The Constitution guarantees him a fair chance for life, liberty, and the pursuit of happiness. But—

> "who would be free
> Themselves must strike the blow."

If he insists upon thrusting his neck under the yoke, he must drag the load. If he insists upon toughening the natural tenderness of the budding orator till it is callous to his squirming, he must sit under him to the bitter end. If he begins by sitting courteously under the considerate Smith, if he sits submissively under the judicious Jones, if he sits cheerfully and with manifest approbation under the witty Robinson, he has forged his own gyves, and in due time, victim of an artificial duty, must sit and sit, without remonstrance or revolt, under the inexorable Jenkins, who never has anything to say, and never knows when to sit down. Slavery was not only bad for the slave, but demoralizing for the slaveholder. It is so in some degree with after-dinner speaking. It is a serious responsibility that each of us takes when he sits consentingly under an after-dinner speaker, since we not only weaken our own powers of resistance, but we help on the abnormal toughening of his. Our safety and his lie in the strength of our resolution to nip him in the bud. We should sit *on* him, not under him. We must crush him while he is still young and tender, that in his age his prolixity may not overwhelm us, nor his ill-advised levity bring reproaches upon himself.

XV

COUSIN ANTHONY'S ADDRESS TO THE TRAINED NURSES

COUSIN ANTHONY'S ADDRESS TO THE TRAINED NURSES.

WOULD you care to read what Cousin Anthony said to the trained nurses? How he came to be permitted to address them I do not know, nor yet how he ventured to undertake such an office; but he did do it, for a newspaper said so, and reported his deliverance at such length and with such an appearance of accuracy, that I cut the report out. Everybody is interested in trained nurses, and everybody likes them, and there may be some readers who have followed Cousin Anthony's meditations on other subjects, who will care to trace the divagations of his intellectuals under the stimulus of an unusual inspiration. So here is his address as the newspaper gave it:—

"One of the managers* of St. Hippocrates Hospital, to whom I divulged my intention of speaking to you to-night, tried hard to turn me from that purpose, reminding me of what, of course, I knew, that there was no information or instruction which it was in my power to give, which could be edifying to so accomplished a band of women as a class of trained nurses about to graduate, or in any way useful to them in their business. But that, while of course it is indisputably obvious, seemed to me to have only this bearing upon the case, that it was a particularly graceful compliment to pay to the class of trained nurses whom I have the honor to address, that a person totally unequipped with technical information should have been permitted to address them. In other years, if I have been rightly informed, it has been the custom to provide such valedictory remarks to the graduating nurses as should tend to impress upon their memories the lessons which they had been taught, and perhaps add some valuable new

* I suspect it was Mrs. Anthony.

ideas to their professional equipment. But with this class it seems to be different. It is conceded that they have learned the business of nursing the sick so thoroughly that no useful last words about it are necessary. No one needs to remind them for the last time not to set the baby on the stove while they are heating the milk, not to confuse quinine with morphine, and not to hold the cork between their teeth while they are pouring the medicine out of the bottle. Very little remains to be done here for the members of this class. To felicitate them upon their calling, to convey to them the expression of a sympathetic admiration for their fortitude and their accomplishments —that is all, except finally to wish them good luck.

"Such last messages as these almost speak themselves. The approval of trained nurses is emphatic, spontaneous, and unanimous. Eli Whitney—I believe it was Eli Whitney—invented the cotton gin, and society thinks well of him. Watt invented the steam locomotive, and Fulton the steamboat, and Morse the telegraph, and Bell the telephone, and society is grateful to them all. Who invented the trained nurse I have never heard, but society's gratitude to that person is intensified by an enthusiasm which none of those other inventors could excite. Doctors have their merits, but you know how it is about doctors. In the first place there are doctors and doctors, and the conditions of doctoring are such that implicit faith in any one of them necessarily implies profound distrust of ninety per cent. of the others. There are different schools of doctors, the primary tenet of each of which is that all the doctors of all the other schools are no good and ought to be abolished by law. It is impossible to secure any unanimity of opinion about doctors even among themselves. A good many people who happen to be enjoying good health go so far as to adopt it as a general principle that it is safest not to have dealings with doctors at all, but to use on occasion such medicines as can be bought ready-made and are recommended in the columns of some unbiassed and reliable newspaper. Indeed, there is such diversity of opinion about doctors, that if there is any ground upon which trained nurses would seem to most people to be best entitled to respectful commiseration, it is because more than half the time they are directly under some doctor's orders, and constrained by the most peremptory obligations to do exactly what he tells them. It used to be the patient who had to do as the doctor said, but nowadays it is the trained nurse, and I am not sure that there is any particular service of hers which is more gratefully esteemed than that which she renders in her capacity of buffer between the doctor and his patient.

"Yes, the doctor is oftentimes disappointing. The community is not quite satisfied with him, and I do not know that it ever will be, for it expects him to know very nearly as much as God, and to exercise very much the same sort of unerring omnipotence; and, after all, that is a good deal to expect of even a carefully educated physician.

"But about the trained nurse there is

really no difference of opinion at all. If a family nowadays has something the matter with it, it sends for the doctor, for doctors will do for an ordinary case. But if its difficulties really become serious it sends for a trained nurse, and then if they don't mend, for another, and if the case is desperate it often gets as many as three; so that it is common practice to measure the dimensions of the pickle which a modern family may happen to be in by the number of trained nurses it takes to get them out of it.

"I wish there was anything about nursing I could hope to tell you, that you do not know already, though that, as I have explained, is the particular thing that I was selected not to do. There is one point that is best gathered from the outside, which it is just possible may have escaped you. When you are walking along the street if you happen to notice a glass jar of milk and a tin cup on a second story window-sill of a house, you need not be surprised to learn, if you inquire, that a new citizen has come to live in that street and that that is the particular house where he is putting up. But inferences based upon such observations as this are not even measurably reliable unless the house looks as if it had one family in it, and a cellar under it; for if it is an apartment-house or a lodging-house, such an appearance as I have noted may signify nothing more than some bachelor's housekeeping.

"I think I should neglect an obvious duty if I omitted to improve such an occasion as this by making a few deprecative suggestions to you relative to the matter of marriage. Of course a good many of you, most of you, no doubt (for all that you know better), will marry sooner or later, and the choice being limited, will marry a man. Now, it is so well understood and so practically recognized in these times that women are the superior beings and know a lot more than men about everything, that for any man to marry any woman has come to be a serious business for him, and one that he undertakes with misgivings and immense trepidation. But if it is fit to scare a man out of all conceit with himself to marry a woman of ordinary accomplishments, just think what it must be to marry a woman with the education of a trained nurse! You must contrive somehow that your exceptional knowledge and experience shall give you exceptional forbearance. Of course you have seen the folly of men in general. Your daily experience with doctors alone, both heretofore and in prospect, will have taught you to appreciate the inevitable disparity between what men think they know and what they really do know. You cannot reasonably expect that the particular men whom you may marry will be materially different from the great mass of their brethren. You must consider, therefore, what it will be for them to spend their lives in daily companionship with an intelligence superior to theirs not only by the accident of sex, but by long discipline and cultivation besides. Be very patient with those men. Their doom is enviable in all the important particulars, and their felicity is almost sure to be great, but while I do not counsel you to make really important concessions to their ignorance, their lot will be all the sunnier if you deal gently with their errors and humor their mistakes. If you make the most of your superiority you may be more instructive, but if you make the least of it they and you both will probably have more fun.

"Among tolerably wise and decent people everywhere I hear one very common complaint. It is that they are too much taken up with their own concerns and do not do enough for other people. The complaint is not merely sentimental, but is the expression of their conviction, that they are missing something that they ought to have. Human happiness is geared to such conditions that if we are to have any considerable share of it we have got to get it at second hand. We cannot often reach out ourselves and grab a great hunk of it. We have to get it through someone else. We may get ready ever so costly and elaborate an apparatus, and expect it to make to order for us all the happiness we can use, but the odds are that the machine won't work. There is no royal road to happiness, any more than there is to learning. The conditions are pretty much alike for all applicants, and each of us must lay in his own store by what means he can. But the nearest thing to a general rule for getting happiness is to help other people. I suppose the reason is that the most important of the things which are at the bottom of happiness is love, and that when we help our fellows we give them, for the time at least, a certain measure of love out of our hearts. I take it to be a great felicity of your vocation that the practice of it is one long exercise of helpfulness, direct, immediate, efficacious. Good works form good characters just as evil deeds form bad. Good works grow on the doer of them, and become habitual just as bad ones do. It seems to me impossible that men or women should do for suffering human creatures what you have learned to do and will do daily, without learning to love humanity and without tasting the happiness that springs from such love and forming the sort of character that grows on such food. There is a great charm to me about the human arm, straight, strong, flexible, ridged

Cousin Anthony to Trained Nurses

with ready muscles and with that wonderfully shifty contrivance, the human hand, at the end of it. And I think the human arm is never so handsome and so admirable as when it comes between the sufferer and the blow, or reaches down, bare and competent, to drag up some downcast creature out of the mire into which he has fallen. The trained nurse is one of the strong arms of our modern society. The very properties of her calling are to sustain the helpless, to draw up the suffering out of their mire of disease. There is no calling more honorable, and there are very few more honored.

"The trained nurse is a brick. We are all her friends, all her admirers, all her debtors. All of us, as we see her here tonight, say God bless her and send her every happiness and success."

IN Mr. E. S. Martin's essays ["Windfalls of Observation." 12mo, $1.25] there is hardly anywhere a thought of learning that comes not out of his individual experience. His humor reads like that of a man to whom things happened just as they seem to in his comments; and sympathy rises as one reads because one feels the memory or the anticipation of similar things. There is, of course, some exaggeration. Horses are not really such quadrupedal embodiments of perversity as Mr. Martin would have us believe. But there are moments even in the life of the most devoted horseman when he might take delight in the words of a writer who doubtless has a preference for solid ground. "A Poet and Not Ashamed" may be deemed an eccentric essay. Nevertheless, it is a wise as well as a witty study on the outward aspect of a great poet. The individual, the personal equation — these are the whole secret of Mr. Martin's skill as an essayist. He may be learned, but he does not need to be. He does what has not been done before.

From the New York Tribune

www.ingramcontent.com/pod-product-compliance
Lightning Source LLC
Chambersburg PA
CBHW021811230426
43669CB00008B/714